Violence in recent Southern fiction

VIOLENCE

in recent

Southern fiction

Louise Y. Gossett

Duke University Press
Durham, N. C.
1965

for Tom

Contents

Introduction

Violence dominates Southern fiction written since 1930. Its boldness sometimes affronts readers, but in the work of substantial writers the shock is not meaningless. Distortions and enlargements emphasize tones, themes, emotions, and relationships which writers in this mode want to make unmistakable. In the hands of second-rate writers this method could be simply an easy way to achieve quick effects. But the vigorous, flexible language and style of the writers discussed here make it evident that they choose their approach deliberately and with high literary consciousness. Their command of technique, moreover, is matched by an ability to meditate on their subjects until they understand them in new and compelling ways. In general terms they are not "popular" authors because their work must be read with concentration and critical effort; it also survives the test of rereading.

Although the violent elements in modern Southern fiction are invariably noted by reviewers and critics, these qualities have not been systematically studied except in an occasional essay. The single full-length study of this subject is Wilbur M. Frohock's *The Novel of Violence in America,* which treats such well-established authors as Steinbeck, Dos Passos, Wolfe, Faulkner, and Caldwell. At present the recent Southern writers have come to attention in studies of the grotesque by William Van O'Connor and Irving Malin, who discuss the symbiotic connection between grotesqueness and violence. Both terms must come into play here, but the latter will be considered the more inclusive.

Violence may be either the inner drive toward the use of

force or the external action of this force. Vehemence, passion, excitability turned inward may immobilize the normal capacities of the person in confusion and tension; turned against another these powers may violate and destroy both the aggressor and the victim. Psychological violence is relayed in states of mind and feelings. Physical violence is the consequence of force exerted by a character against himself or against others, resulting in extreme acts like arson, rape, mutilation, suicide, and murder. At times in current Southern fiction the violent force is the power of nature threatening man in storms, floods, and droughts, or in hostile land. So interrelated are psychological and physical violence, of course, that one is generally the concomitant of the other.

In literature the grotesque connotes incongruity and distortion which emphasize the abnormal in appearance, manners, behavior, setting, and event. The deviation from conditions broadly accepted as normal is so extreme as to call dramatic attention to itself. The direction of this deviation is toward the inharmonious, the ugly, the repulsive, and the unsavory. For the moment the common levels of human action are raised—or lowered—to the bizarre, the absurd, and the horrible.

Both violence and grotesqueness are dramatizations of disorder. And just as the negative implies the positive—grief, joy and evil, good—disorder argues order. In the most comprehensive perspective, violence is part of the acute criticism to which Western writers in the twentieth century have subjected their culture. It is also part of the total response of creative artists to jarring changes in man's view of himself. Affected by theories of evolution and psychoanalysis and faced by the threats of automation, the totalitarian state, and nuclear annihilation, the thinking man has questioned both his humanity and his being. He has been torn between feeling either that his culture has failed him or that he has failed his culture. He does not ask for the recovery of the old order but for the rediscovery of order itself. Patently, Southern writers are touched by these currents, and the broad contours of violence and grotesqueness in their work are shaped by them. In addition, local qualities in the South seem to give particular direction to violence in contemporary fiction by writers from this region. The abstractions which can be discussed as tradition, philosophic temper, social values, and religious principles become fiction, of course, only when transmuted into character, conflict, action, narration, and mood. These specifications, however, take their coloring from the milieu. The richness and complication of Southern history and manners are thus a benefit to the essential creative play for writers between their sense of home and of the world, between their private problems and those publicly displayed in characters, between their involvement in their material and their detachment from it.

In the development of this study I have profited especially from the thoughtful suggestions of Dr. Arlin Turner. Grants from the Danforth Foundation and from Duke University in co-operation with the Woodrow Wilson Foundation generously freed my time for research and the initial preparation of this material. I am indebted to the Duke University Graduate Committee on Publications for an award which made possible the publication of this book.

To my parents, Mr. and Mrs. J. B. Young, who made their farm, Bunger's Mill, available to me as a summer workshop, I owe special thanks.

Louise Y. Gossett

San Antonio, Texas
January 31, 1965

Part One

The climate of violence: Wolfe, Caldwell, Faulkner

Southern writers who began to publish fiction in the forties had as their immediate literary background in the South the writing of three men who dealt with violence: Thomas Wolfe, Erskine Caldwell, and William Faulkner. There is no intention here of exhausting all that might be said about violence in the fiction of these three or of establishing incontestable lines of influence from any one writer to another. It will be sufficient simply to indicate primary sources for certain kinds of violence and to analyze the use made of this material. For this purpose illustrations will come chiefly from the work which Wolfe, Caldwell, and Faulkner had published by 1940. Individual as their work is, it contains in common a view of life which could be expressed forcefully by violent or grotesque characters and situations. By treating such themes as frustration and loneliness, economic exploitation, bondage to the past, defilement of the land, and the flux of time, and by experimenting with language and form, these men opened new literary approaches to the experience of the South.

To define conclusively this pervasive but intangible experience and to assess its influence on writers living within the region is impossible. Speculation, however, can suggest that certain elements in the experience might reappear in literature as violence. In the past there are a westward moving frontier, a relatively stable agrarian society on the settled land, and the Civil War and Reconstruction. The turbulence of the frontier fathered a lusty humor which has had a long literary life. The aristocratic ideal of power vested in ownership of the land established a social code which offered Southern writers an American equivalent of manners as a subject of fiction. Having suffered military defeat and occupation, the region holds a bitter memory of violence. Furthermore, the despair which accompanied failure, the collapse of responsible leadership, the glorification of the military, and the private assumption of force to restore an order based on white supremacy seeded the future for acts of violence.

In addition to the events of history, the arts of political speaking and writing stamped Southern expression with a characteristic extravagance. A respect for rhetoric permeated all social classes. Public oratory was a cohesive agent when occasion brought people together. It was useful in developing and spreading the myth of the Old South after the war, for it established in public the mood and memory to which many would subscribe. Their commemoration of the past bolstered their confidence in the future.

Nor was the embellishment of language confined to politics; it appeared also in sermons, newspaper columns, correspondence, conversation, and belles-lettres. It was part of the tradition of manners which the planter society was attempting to establish. A substantial polysyllabic richness of expression further characterized the romantic literary tradition as exemplified in Poe. Such a flourishing convention of rhetoric and eloquence may well stimulate hyperbole and violence in the use of language.

In this group of three writers, Faulkner and Caldwell dealt especially with the violence inherent in the traditions and conflicts coming into the present from Southern history. Faulkner and Wolfe in particular lavished eloquent and often extravagant language upon their conceptions. By demonstrating that violence in characters and incidents had structural, symbolic, and thematic importance, the three prepared a climate of violence for their successors. Not the least of their contributions was to train an audience to read stories of violence and to expect more than sensationalism. The extent of their influence is not the issue here. The new Southern writers of the past two decades have been too independent and original to follow slavishly their predecessors. They themselves would be the first to disclaim membership in a "school." Nevertheless, they inherited a literary achievement in violence which could not be ignored.

1

From 1930 to 1940 the work of Thomas Wolfe poured out in giant volumes, the length and laxness of the novels being affronts to the conventions of structure for twentieth-century American fiction. Dos Passos' *U.S.A.* was a triology of manageable volumes, but Wolfe thought in terms of six novels eventually to carry the history of the Gant and Pentland families from 1791 to 1933. Wolfe's death in 1938 cut short the project. With the posthumous publication of *The Web and the Rock* (1939) and *You Can't Go Home Again* (1940), he left a tetralogy which chronicles the development of Eugene Gant and George Webber, personae for Thomas Wolfe. Because Wolfe's work is directly autobiographical, it has been possible for a careful scholar like Floyd C. Watkins to discover in the Wolfe family and in Asheville newspapers and city records the sources of characters and events in the fiction.[1] The authenticity of the violence which occurs in Wolfe's fiction, however, makes it no more compelling than is the violence derived from more subtly transmuted experiences in the work of other Southern writers.

Briefly, the chronicle *Look Homeward, Angel* (1929) takes Eugene from birth to college against a background dominated by his bacchanalian father W. O. Gant and his puritanical

1. See *Thomas Wolfe's Characters: Portraits from Life* (Norman: University of Oklahoma Press, 1957).

mother Eliza Pentland. In *Of Time and the River* (1935) young Gant escapes from home to Harvard and to Europe; in *The Web and the Rock* the young man, now named George Webber, returns to New York for a career of writing and teaching and for his love affair with Esther Jack. Webber's unhappy attempts to return to Esther Jack, to his boyhood home, and to Europe in *You Can't Go Home Again* prove to him that although the past shapes the present, the past is irrecoverable. Each novel is a memorial to violence in one of the ages of man.

Not since Whitman had an American writer appeared with such an omnivorous appetite for human experience. This desire to multiply immediate sense impressions, to extend experience through endless reading, and to write millions of words in order to preserve everything that had ever happened to him drove Wolfe mercilessly. The expression of this compulsion through Eugene Gant and George Webber is the source of the inner violence which shakes these young men and hurls them through life to near-madness. Their torrential outpouring, it is assumed, is Wolfe's own celebration of food and drink, spring and fall, love and hate, city and village, crowds, trains, and deserted streets; his own revulsion from an insensitive family and an unjust social order.

Wolfe takes the passionate view of life which has been ascribed to Southerners.[2] Living must be an exercise of the senses, an insatiable appetite for the range of human experience with the energy and stamina to participate fully. The intellectualizing of perception comes only after the color or sound, the grief or joy, the serenity or violence have been so profoundly felt that the mind can in no way falsify their essence. For thus insisting upon the validity of what is felt as well as what is thought, the Southerner has been labeled a romantic. Neither in Wolfe nor in any of the recent major Southern writers, however, does this quality run to sentimen-

2. For a concise formulation of this view see Herbert Marshall McLuhan, "The Southern Quality," *Southern Review*, LV (July, 1947), 360-361.

tality. There is a counterbalancing tragic view of life. In the midst of gorging on experience, Wolfe's characters sense that frustration, failure, and defeat are inevitable because the human is the limited. Man may rage, but he cannot escape the passage of time and the prison of self. The richness of change which time brings is also a bewildering moment-by-moment alteration of impressions. The demands of the self for definition amount to a frenzied assault on any door which it seems might open onto order and integrity. Thwarted and disappointed, man howls imprecations and batters his way to another door.

In Wolfe's novels the tensions which rack the hero Gant-Webber in his search are violent in themselves and generate violence. Gant-Webber often acts hysterically, fluctuating between heights and depths like a manic-depressive. Largely a self-portrait of Wolfe, he vibrates between the polarities of love and hate, acceptance and rejection, certainty and doubt, courage and cowardice. Every tremor shoots off violence like a Roman candle. Even when Wolfe describes rather than dramatizes the moods of Gant-Webber, the quantity of detail creates an impression of impassioned feeling surging throughout the novels. The expression of this violence by character and language is shaped in part by the people and the idiom of Wolfe's Southern background. One problem with which Wolfe never ceased to struggle was how to separate himself from Gant-Webber in order to give the young man's struggle an independent dramatic existence. Wolfe was increasingly short-circuited by introspection. He needed to relate the violence to a society in which it can mean more than merely the death pangs of adolescence.

Amply provided with the materials of violence, Wolfe has difficulty using them dramatically. Often he prefers description or exposition to enactment. The omniscient author, for example, declares that at Harvard, Eugene suffered a hunger "so literal, cruel and physical that it wanted to devour the earth and all the things and people in it, and when it failed in this attempt, his spirit would drown in an ocean of horror and desolation. . . ."[3] Having asserted this Faustian appetite, Wolfe then neglects to embody it in any action more furious than reading thousands of books or ranging the streets of Boston, greedily peering into faces and listening to conversations. When the young Faustus, now imaged as Jason, reaches Paris, he prowls the streets "like a maddened animal." Unable to consume the complexities of life, he was "caught in the toils of that insatiate desire, that terrible devouring hunger that grew constantly from what it fed upon and that drove him blindly to madness."[4] Throughout the novel the violence promised by the fury remains in the telling, not in the doing. The rage as a constant element in the characterization of Eugene rarely subsides, but it becomes static by repetition because it opens no new understanding of Eugene to himself or to the reader. Finally it turns into Eugene's single decisive act—writing. But even this is an undisciplined flinging down in wild and broken phrases of a picture of his homesickness. As the center of the novel the anger provides emotional unity, but the structural effect is a whirlwind. The movement includes no resolution; it merely circles the fact of frustration again and again.

The second of Wolfe's angry young men is George Webber. In *The Web and the Rock* he passes through a childhood and college career similar to Eugene Gant's and on to the crisis of a love affair. Here the violence is psychological and verbal. When Webber's paranoiac tendencies get out of hand, he blames Esther Jack for the persecutions he imagines he endures. She has given Webber the stability of her affection and passion, her joy in being an artist, and her faith in his talent. But when he feels that her mistress-mother role threatens his integrity as an artist and a man, he struggles against her. Their quarrels thunder in a violence which is again a matter of language. George shouts in a "convulsion of

3. *Of Time and the River: A Legend of Man's Hunger in His Youth* (New York: Sun Dial Press, 1944), pp. 91-92.
4. *Ibid.*, p. 660.

mad, mindless fury."[5] Wolfe's meticulous record of the snarled sentences, the simple inanities of daily conversation blown up into crashing disagreements, and the insults to family and friends captures the embarrassment of being human and therefore irrational, petty, and childish. The violence defeats love. And when nothing is left except the fury, George flees to Europe.

Webber's frustration is more complex than that of Eugene Gant in *Of Time and the River*, being compounded of exhaustion after three years of work on his book, of despair that the great man-swarm wastes itself in fears and littleness of spirit, of rebellion against the web that women can weave around men, and of hatred for himself for succumbing to the demonic. He is seized not with mere fury but with madness. The violence of the seizures, as was true of the fury, lies in Wolfe's image-shaping language:

It soaked first into the deep folds and convolutions of his brain its damnable slime of poison, and then it channeled out its blackened tongues along the veins and arteries of his flesh. It heated and inflamed his brain with a dull, sweltering fire that was like a smear of blood and murder, but all else within the house of the flesh it chilled, froze, and constricted with a reptile's fang.[6]

Finally it is the physical violence of a drunken brawl at the Munich *Oktoberfest* which restores George to sanity. He sees the mirror reflection of his battered face as an image of his manhood which reconciles the warring Body and Man: "He knew that we who are men are more than men, and less than spirit. What have we but the pinion of a broken wing to soar half-heavenward!"[7] Because the quarrel of Webber the artist with the world is mixed with nothing more than the pangs of belated adolescence, the violence of the portrayal is a documentary detail rather than a commentary on the theme of the suffering artist.

    5. *The Web and the Rock* (New York: Harper's Modern Classics, 1958), p. 560.
    6. *Ibid.*, p. 548.
    7. *Ibid.*, p. 693.

The inner violence which accompanies the anger, hate, disgust, scorn, and despair of youth is most fully presented in Eugene's rebellion against the Gants in *Look Homeward, Angel.* The rejection of the family is both aesthetic and moral. The house where Eugene was born and Dixieland, the boardinghouse to which his mother later moves, are cheap and ugly. The manners and conversation of the family are crude. No effort is made to give life any touch of grace, dignity, and joy. Eugene is ashamed of the vulgar perversity of his family, of "the waste, the confusion, the blind cruelty of their lives."[8]

His mother Eliza repulses him with her hoarding of useless odds and ends, her pleasure in the commotion of litigation, her meandering tales of success and disaster. Her violence stems from blind selfishness incapable of understanding any view of life but its own. She sacrifices herself, her husband, and her children to her greed for property and justifies her avarice by the firmest of middle-class convictions: economic security is the chief end of man's duty. She flourishes while her husband disintegrates and her children struggle for love and consideration. Obtuse to the point of being evil, although not intentionally malevolent, Eliza is unmoved by the violence which she provokes.

In contrast to the meanness of Eliza, Eugene's father is built on a grandiose scale. His violence signifies the capacity to spend oneself. A man of colossal appetites and energy, W. O. Gant storms through life abusing himself and others because he can find nothing complete enough to express the sense of glory in him. Even Eliza recognizes that "insensate and cruel as he had often been," there was some greatness in "the enormous beating color of his life."[9]

For most of the time that he appears in *Look Homeward, Angel* and *Of Time and the River*, W. O. Gant is a physical wreck, crippled by inflammatory rheumatism and tortured by

8. *Look Homeward, Angel: A Story of the Buried Life* (New York: Modern Library), p. 137.
9. *Ibid.*, p. 19.

cancer, but his vitality charges the scenes with violence. On a drunken rampage he may stagger into Dixieland, kicking over Eugene and scattering boarders until his daughter Helen quiets him. His invective resounds through the novels. He howls that the Pentlands have destroyed his peace of mind, that Eliza is a fiend out of hell, that his children are ungrateful, brutish beasts, that his son Steve is a "fearful, cruel, and accursed reprobate," and that the widow who rents part of his Woodson Street house has drunk his heart's-blood and gloated over his misery.[10] Everything Gant touches becomes enlarged —the fires he builds, the vegetables he grows, the pain he suffers, the frustration he endures. This exaggeration intensifies the father image for Eugene. On his first trip to Harvard the young man remembers the feeling of security imparted by his father's violence:

Oh, to hear him prowling like a wakened lion below, the stertorous hoarse frenzy of his furious breath; to hear the ominous muttering mounting to faint howls as with infuriated relish he prepared the roaring invective of the morning's tirade, to hear him muttering as the coal went rattling out upon the fire, to hear him growling as savagely the flame shot up the trembling chimney-throat, to hear him muttering back and forth like a raging beast, finally to hear his giant stride racing through the house prepared now, storming to the charge, and the well-remembered howl of his awakened fury as springing to the door-way of the back-room stairs he flung it open, yelling at them to awake.[11]

The Gant family is all but a travesty of the affectionate clan which others project as the Southern family. Nothing of the formality made possible by wealth and leisure, servants and space restrains their rivalry and spite. The tensions, although not finally destructive for Eugene, delay and warp his maturity.

When Wolfe uses incidents of violence which are external to his hero and family, they seem like set pieces of description,

10. *Ibid.*, pp. 247, 287.
11. *Of Time and the River*, p. 29.

admirably composed but isolated in the text. These episodes are less prolix and lyrical than are the passages dominated by the personality of the characters—or the author. The fact that they first appear in *The Web and the Rock* may be the result of Wolfe's attempt to create a character less closely identified with his own sensibility than is Eugene. They also indicate a new interest in delineating the social scene. Witnessing a fatal accident fixes in the young George Webber's mind the terror and ugliness of life. On the other hand, killing people is treated as an everyday exercise by George's part-Cherokee friend Nebraska Crane, whose father is a policeman. Bras blandly notes that his father is always killing people. With something of Mark Twain's double-barreled understatement he reports a conversation between his father and his mother in which his father suddenly remembers, " 'Oh, yes! I clean forgot to tell you! I had to shoot a nigger today!' 'That so?' my maw says. 'Is there any other news?' "[12] Listening to Bras's stories of murder is another step in the educative process of violence in George's life. George learns from violence as Eugene Gant never does.

When Wolfe began increasingly to objectify his material, the violence gained a social context. The growth of George Webber through the action of his community comes in the story of the Negro, Dick Prosser. This sequence is the only extended development of violence in Wolfe's novels which involves a Negro. It is significant that Wolfe treats the incident as impersonal and self-contained. He presents no detailed account of the friction between races, no record of prolonged brooding by an outraged young man, no sociology of inequities. Hints are sufficient. He can count on the heritage of violence, actual or potential, which belongs to every community where black and white do not meet as human beings to complicate implicitly the tension and disillusion which explode in the action. In *Look Homeward, Angel*, Eugene and his

12. *The Web and the Rock*, p. 41.

friends learn to harass Negroes without hating them, for "it was proper to cuff these people kindly, curse them cheerfully, feed them magnanimously."[13] With exemplary patience, Dick Prosser, a war veteran, fulfils the part required of him. But then he goes berserk and terrorizes the town. By the time the posse catches up with him, he has murdered nine men. The deputies empty their ammunition into him and hang the riddled body in the undertaker's window for the townspeople to see. The boys who had admired Dick take their shuddering look at the body and listen to the bragging deputies. Bras Crane makes the only overt comment of social criticism. He disparages the boasts of these men: "*We* killed a big one! *We* —we killed a b'ar, we did!"[14] To Wolfe himself Dick is inexplicable, something out of "the dark heart of the secret and undiscovered South . . . a symbol of man's evil innocence . . . a projection of his own unfathomed quality, a friend, a brother, and a mortal enemy, an unknown demon . . . two worlds together—a tiger and a child."[15]

The details of this account come directly from an actual case in Asheville. But Wolfe made a significant addition which Floyd Watkins cites.[16] By combining three Negroes in the character of Dick Prosser, Wolfe achieved the ambiguity which makes the Negro more than a man of violence. The virtues of Prosser were those of the janitor of Bingham Academy; the ability to mesmerize his listeners was that of a Negro preacher in Asheville; the violence was that of a desperado who terrorized the town. Complete within itself, the episode, although expertly and powerfully presented, remains a separate piece in the novel.

Only in the last of the posthumous novels, *You Can't Go Home Again*, does Wolfe link violence specifically with the American social scheme and finally with the nature of man.

13. *Look Homeward, Angel*, p. 96.
14. *The Web and the Rock*, p. 154.
15. *Ibid.*, p. 156.
16. *Thomas Wolfe's Characters*, pp. 104-108.

The stock market crash in 1929 and the subsequent depression signified to Webber that America had allowed wealth, graft, special privilege, and intellectual dishonesty to corrupt her ideal of freedom, tolerance, and justice. In Libya Hill (and Asheville) the real estate boom reflects the general corruption of the country, and blind Judge Rumford Bland epitomizes inherently evil man. In New York the anonymity represented by the apartment building in which Esther Jack lives comes to violence in the suicide of C. Green, "average" American. Only by death can Green distinguish himself from the "Concentrated Blotters" who hurry by on the subway, nameless atoms swarming with the crowd. "But now, observe him!" Wolfe exclaims over the corpse. "No longer is he just 'another guy'—already he has become a 'special guy'—he has become '*The* Guy.' C. Green at last has turned into a—*Man!*"[17]

George Webber witnesses a similar kind of dehumanization during his last visit to Germany in 1936. His friends hate one another out of fear of what their association may mean politically. Watching horrified while German officers remove from his compartment a Jew trying to escape from the country, George feels ashamed and guilty before this man whom he now identifies as a brother. Like C. Green, the Jew becomes a man to the nameless crowd only when he is singled out by violence. Not only does his treatment express the depravity of Hitlerism, but it also manifests the "primitive spirit of greed and lust and force" which has always plagued man.[18] This fact of omnipresent violence, however, does not lead to despair. If Webber's "Credo" to his editor Foxhall Edwards at the end of *You Can't Go Home Again* is read as Wolfe's testament of faith to his editor Maxwell Perkins, then Wolfe believes that man can control his barbarism. And after death there is a greater love, a greater life, and a kinder home which "here on the pillars of this earth are founded, toward which

17. *You Can't Go Home Again* (New York: Grosset's Universal Library, 1940), p. 479.
18. *Ibid.*, p. 705.

the conscience of the world is tending—a wind is rising, and the rivers flow."[19] He did not live to show how this hope might have affected his treatment of violence and disorder in the life of man.

What he did show was that the lyrical and the violent could mutually support one another. His celebration of growing up in the South and discovering the world beyond is compounded of verbal tension and emotional contrarieties. Sentences inundate the reader with their length. Series of nouns name each nuance of experience. Torrents of adjectives and adverbs qualify the naming. Nothing emerges life-size. It is doubled by words which surge along in parallel rhythms.

Wolfe's capacity for total recall and his verbal energy have been alternately acclaimed as the gifts of genius and condemned as the faults of immaturity.[20] The believing reader takes the words as tokens of genuine emotion; the disbelieving dismisses them as substitutes. Sustained emotionalism such as Wolfe essayed is perhaps an impossibility. It is least convincing when used as the narrator's choral comment on action in the novel; it is most authentic when incorporated in the characterization, as when young Eugene discovers beauty and pain or when W. O. Gant curses his household and his fate. Violence is a by-product of the intense determination of the adolescent to wrench from every experience its limits of sensation and meaning. It is expressed in the language of a tormented youth describing his inner confusion: "The trick was," George Webber comments, "to get his reason and his emotions pulling together in double harness, instead of letting them fly off in opposite directions, tearing him apart between them."[21] The exaggeration, the exuberance, and the excess of

19. *Ibid.*, p. 743.
20. The best single source of a history of the criticism of Wolfe is *The Enigma of Thomas Wolfe*, ed. Richard Walser (Cambridge: Harvard University Press, 1953), where are collected such essays as Bernard De Voto's "Genius Is Not Enough" and Thomas Lyle Collins' "Wolfe's Genius vs. His Critics."
21. *You Can't Go Home Again*, p. 6.

this conflict, which seems to be Wolfe's own, dictate the excited treatment given the characters and incidents. Violence in this kind of enlargement functions more directly in Wolfe as a revelation of the author's personality than it does in Faulkner or Caldwell.

2

From the first, Erskine Caldwell used the subject of social disorder which Wolfe had begun to explore only at the end of his career. Social criticism—at least in the form of social unease—permeates much of Caldwell's work, particularly that written during the thirties. At this time, in addition to fiction, he published *Some American People* (1935) and *You Have Seen Their Faces* (1937), reports on the dispossessed worker in the United States. Having found a salable formula for his fiction, Caldwell has continued to publish novels and short stories with predictable characters and events. Later novels—*A House in the Uplands* (1946), *The Sure Hand of God* (1947), *Place Called Estherville* (1949), and *Episode in Palmetto* (1950)—continue the series which he calls a "cycloramic depiction of the South."[22] These books are populated by decadent families, prostitutes with varying degrees of crude honor, murderers, and corrupted children, figures who lack the inner consistency and carefully reproduced Southern idiom which gives characters in his early novels a recognizable if a less than engaging individuality.

The accuracy with which Caldwell reported sociological conditions is verifiable. But when he translates into novels and short stories facts about land impoverished by cotton growing and people exploited by tenant farming, sharecropping, and mill work, the fiction is violent, flamboyant, and gro-

22. Erskine Caldwell, *Call It Experience: The Years of Learning How to Write* (New York: Duell, Sloan and Pearce, 1951), p. 181.

tesque. About the violence Caldwell made no apology. In an interview he asserted that the South is a violent country:

I've seen a man beat a mule to death because the sun was hot and he was tired and tense, sick of the endless sameness of his life. I've been in a barnyard at the end of a day in the cotton fields when the boss came over to ask why a mule was lame. A Negro explained that the mule had stepped in a rabbit hole. The boss beat the Negro unconscious—knowing the Negro couldn't fight back. I've been an unwilling witness at a number of lynchings.[23]

He also indicated that he intended his work to teach as well as to entertain. He does not have to say that lynching and cruelty are wrong. He can activate consciences "by showing people oppressed to hopelessness and impoverished to hopelessness. . . ."[24] In *Call It Experience,* the autobiography of his writing, Caldwell mentions his observation of rural Georgia counties made during trips with the local physician and the tax assessor. When in 1927 he left the Atlanta *Journal* to write fiction, he was determined "to write about Southern life as I knew it."[25]

The comments do not mean that Caldwell made a transcript of Southern life, but they do indicate that his concern for problems in the South was in the beginning serious. "I wanted," he declares, "to tell the story of the people I knew in the manner in which they actually lived their lives from day to day and year to year, and to tell it without regard for fashions in writing and traditional plots."[26] In fact, the very extremity of his concern may have betrayed him into exaggerations which defeated his purpose. The reduction of human complexities to economic or political exploitation increases the amount of violence but reduces its impact.

The plot in most of Caldwell's early novels is a social problem so far advanced that it either threatens to or actually does

23. Quoted in Robert Van Gelder, "A Talk with Erskine Caldwell," *Writers and Writing* (New York: Charles Scribner's Sons, 1946), p. 35.
24. Van Gelder, p. 37.
25. *Call It Experience,* p. 48.
26. *Ibid.,* p. 101.

destroy the characters. No character, however, blames himself for his condition; the fault lies with the landlord, the loan company, the mill owner, the merchant who refuses credit, or the politician. And failing all these, there is God Himself. The problem is formulated in almost doctrinaire terms. The accompanying narrow view of human beings tends to squeeze out their humanity altogether.

In *Tobacco Road* (1932) Caldwell preaches that Captain John should have taught his tenants better methods of farming instead of abandoning them to starve without the equipment and the credit to make a crop. The condition of the poor white as well as the Negro has preoccupied Caldwell. Historically, both groups were subject to the apathy of malnutrition, disease, and fatigue brought on by inadequate food, improper sanitation, and long work hours. Unschooled, these people were suspicious and distrustful. The poor white, it is true, had status in his color. By this virtue he could subscribe to the code of white supremacy. Although the refinements of plantation life never filtered through to him, he could claim the myth. He might also possess the independence of the frontiersman jealous of his self-reliance and his belongings. In Caldwell's fiction, however, the poor white has become a physiological automaton. Jeeter Lester treads the daily squirrel cage of scrabbling for food, yelling at Dude for "chunking" a baseball against the sagging house, and trying to patch enough inner tubes to get his old car into town in the forlorn hope of selling a load of worthless wood. His ignorance of how to care for the land finally destroys him when the fire set to burn over his fields also burns his tinderbox cabin.

The defeat, actual or threatened, of man by economic change is one of the most productive sources of violence for Southern writers. It is possible, of course, to read the whole history of sectionalism in the United States as a conflict between agricultural and industrial economies. This conflict engages writers who want to define the consequences of the kinds of answers given to the question whether the ultimate value is the profit or the person, the increase in capital, or the relation of the work to the worker. Following the economic collapse of the South after the Civil War, it seemed to men like Henry Grady that industry would solve Southern problems. The region needed to diversify its economy in order to minimize agricultural depressions and to secure funds for needed services like education, but whether a radical shift in the economic basis of the South would destroy more than it would construct has been a continuing argument. The fear is that industrialism will destroy the individuality, the rural virtues, the graciousness of the South; the hope is that it will make all prosperous.

Whatever the gain or loss, social and economic dislocations —the substance of violence—have been inevitable. These at times have manifested themselves in urban slums, unhealthful working conditions, strikes, new competition between white and Negro, the disintegration of family bonds, a decline of church and community controls over behavior, and the substitution of the relativism and materialism of science for the teleology of religious faith. This welter of conflict is the matrix for much of the violence which recent Southern writers have portrayed. The collision of inherited agrarianism and its peculiar social institutions and philosophy with industrialism challenges the Southerner either to defend or to attack the inheritance. By using violent people and acts, grotesque exaggerations of appearance and behavior, and contorted diction, the writer testifies to his own shock and goads the reader into paying attention to the implications of the changes.

In *God's Little Acre* (1933) and *Tragic Ground* (1944) Caldwell makes the factory and the lure of cash the enemy. The corruption of the farm and the town is embodied in Ty Ty Walden and his son-in-law Will Thompson. On the land, Ty Ty is not a devoted agrarian like Jeeter Lester. Instead of farming he digs for gold. Avarice toward the land is also avarice toward God, for the acre set aside as a tithe is so mobile that a gold strike would never have to be shared with the church. In town, Will Thompson leads the workers to oppose arbitration to end the strike at the textile mill. The threatened violence of the workers seems indecisive beside the power of the mill owners. Company police shoot Will in the back. The Douthits of rural Beaseley County occupy tragic ground when Spence is laid off at a wartime powder plant and the family is caught in Poor Boy, a slum of shacks where uprooted war workers live. The bumbling efforts of the Welfare Department to rehabilitate the Douthits caricature bureaucracy. Spence's son-in-law Jim Howard instructs the welfare worker: "If you want to do the right thing, you ought to put all the blame on Poor Boy. . . . The finest folks in the world would get mean and bad if they had to live in a place like this."[27]

Such social determinism is implied throughout Caldwell's work. The degrading external pressures which Caldwell detects serve him twice. They are a simple and inclusive explanation of the nature of his ravaged characters, and they prescribe a violent mode of expression. Thus both motivation and style are inherent in the view which Caldwell takes.

In addition to portraying what happens when the poor Southern white denies the land and goes into the factory, Caldwell makes use of the chief cause of violence within the social organization of the South itself—the relation between Negro and white. Between the two, any action, whether the official course of state or local governments or the private move of a citizen, has been able to claim justification if it were advanced as a buttress to white domination. During and following Reconstruction, violence against a Negro was satisfying because it defied the Yankee intruder and it asserted the power of the Southern white.

The most publicized form of racial violence has been lynching. This kind of mob violence takes over more often in the South than in other regions; nearly 90 per cent of the 1,886

27. *Tragic Ground* (New York: Duell, Sloan and Pearce, 1944), p. 236.

lynchings committed in the United States from 1900 through 1930 took place in the Southern states.[28] The highest incidence of lynching from 1882 to 1956 occurred in Mississippi, where 537 Negroes and 40 whites were lynched.[29] Since 1935 the rate has dropped, some years being reported free of such incidents. Improved local law enforcement and federal assistance with state investigations have helped to curb this lawlessness.

The focus of the Southerner's insecurity after the Civil War became not slave insurrection but what Wilbur J. Cash calls the rape complex.[30] The high position of the woman set apart to preserve the purity of the Anglo-Saxon became a symbol of the superiority of the white Southerner. The taboo against sexual relations between white women and black men was absolute. To lynch a Negro for attacking a white woman was not lawless violence but chivalric protection of the future. No amount of rational discussion about the little likelihood of rape could allay this inflammable anxiety. Caldwell uses violence most trenchantly when he deals with rape and mob hysteria in *Trouble in July*. In the novel the sheriff clearly acts out the intent of public opinion: lynch law alone should apply when black rapes white. Political expediency is systemized to let violence win.

The fact that an innocent Negro jail prisoner is abducted by the mob as a substitute for the culprit involves Sheriff Jeff McCurtain personally in the case because "Sam Brinson is a sort of special friend of mine, even if he is a colored man. I just couldn't stand having something bad happen to him."[31] McCurtain rescues Sam but fumbles until Sonny Clark is lynched. The shock of hearing Katy Barlow confess that she had lied about being raped and of seeing her stoned to death

28. Harrington C. Brearley, "The Pattern of Violence," *Culture in the South*, ed. William T. Couch (Chapel Hill: University of North Carolina Press, 1934), p. 312.

29. From the Department of Records and Research at Tuskegee Institute reported in *World Almanac and Book of Facts*, 1958, p. 312.

30. *The Mind of the South* (New York: Alfred A. Knopf, 1941), pp. 114-117.

31. *Trouble in July* (New York: Duell, Sloan and Pearce, 1940), p. 177.

by the same men who earlier had eyed her lustfully, jolts the Sheriff into recalling his oath of public office to perform his duty "without fear or favor." "I reckon I had sort of forgotten it," he remarks in a burst of self-awareness given to few of Caldwell's characters.[32]

McCurtain, who to himself and his friends seems an acceptable, likeable person, shows in the glare of violence as a bumbler whose ineptness threatens the political order of the state. Caldwell's incompetents are undeterred not only by law but also by religion. They reflect the intellectual conservatism and the radical emotionalism of the Bible Belt. In them the fervor which brought Protestant missionaries to the frontier to quicken and convert the sinners has degenerated into self-indulgence. Their background is the groups of unlettered, superstitious poor whites and Negroes who listened to hellfire-and-brimstone preachers. Luridly drawn pictures of sin and damnation have about them the glamor of the forbidden, and more than one congregation has been titillated by graphic references to human weakness. The juxtaposition of spiritual impulses and sexual satisfactions in orgiastic religious demonstrations has provided Caldwell and other Southern writers a fruitful source of commentary on the violent, erratic behavior of man.

In *Journeyman,* characters with travesties of names enact a religious experience in the mode of a tall tale. Caldwell, however, says that he had often observed counterparts of his chief character in Georgia, Florida, and the Carolinas, and the story he considers "one of the indigenous phases of life in the South."[33] Semon Dye, an itinerant lay preacher, has a riverboat gambler's way with liquor, loaded dice, and women. After winning everything his host Clay Horey possesses, including his wife, he conducts a revival, a festival of sex. For people isolated on dreary, unproductive bits of farms, the violence is too welcome a change to be disapproved. Clay

32. *Ibid.*, p. 241.
33. *Call It Experience*, p. 155.

pities the next folk to fall victim to Semon, but he admits, "I reckon they'll be just as tickled to have him around as I was."[34]

Clearly, Caldwell finds in rural Georgia and other parts of the South situations which indict the social order, but often he lets the violence which should sharpen the indictment become so exaggerated that it dulls the effect. Caldwell eases the reader into his material by comedy in the early tradition of broad oral folk humor, lustily biological in content. This method might be a clever presentation of violence in the idiom of the country people to convince the reader of the need for reform; the comedy goes astray, however, when entertaining incongruities become monstrous absurdities and caricatures which are horrible and repulsive rather than amusing. As the situations and characters approach these extremes, the social indictment falters. If the comedy alone is the point, then the social zeal is too prominent. The reader has to work harder to feel satisfied that he knows what the author's purpose is, and lacking this satisfaction he may dismiss the fiction as mere sensationalism.

The plight of the countryman in the city, for example, is a theme open to comic, satiric, or tragic development. In *Tobacco Road* the encounter is handled lightly. The marriage of Sister Bessie, widow and purveyor of her private religion called "Holy," and Dude, Jeeter's sixteen-year-old son, in Augusta is a comedy of errors. From the clerk's stumbling explanation, Bessie confuses venereal diseases with mites. She objects to paying a two-dollar fee for getting married, which is the Lord's doings anyway. But she and the clerk good-humoredly satisfy the official forms. Later, when Bessie, Jeeter, and Dude bring a load of wood to town to sell, they treat themselves to a dingy hotel room and innocently expose Bessie. She spends the night being shunted from room to room, enjoying this strange hotel life. "It ain't like it is out on the tobacco road," she tells Jeeter.

The sketches in *Georgia Boy* (1943) maintain this joking

34. *Journeyman* (New York: Penguin Books, Inc., 1947), p. 137.

mood. The poor, lazy, illiterate Southern white in these stories is Pa Stroup, whose cunning is beguiling. He schemes, lies, and steals his way in and out of encounters with paper baling machines, silk tie salesladies, gypsies, lively grass widows, and cockfighting. In the background his wife bends over the wash-pot with which she earns a living for the improvident family. The life of their Negro handyman, Handsome Brown, who, like all the Negroes in Caldwell's fiction, does the unpleasant work—whether it be chasing goats from the ridgepole of the house or substituting as a feeding ground for woodpeckers to keep the night silent for Pa's sleep—is treated for humor rather than social criticism. Underneath this humor, however, is the misery of poverty and racial discrimination which Caldwell portrays directly in other works. Irony informs the advice of Uncle Ned Stroup, recently escaped from the penitentiary. He charges his nephew:

There's so many of us in the world nowadays that one of us is apt to get out of hand every now and then, but that don't mean that the rest of the Stroups ain't the finest people God ever made. You just go ahead and be a good Stroup like I told you.[35]

In these instances ignorance and innocence are amusing and are not blown up into Gothic horrors, but the rollicking life can also be read as social criticism.

Violence operates best in Caldwell at this level. When the characters become involved in destructive acts of murder and arson, Caldwell overtaxes their single dimension. Spence Douthit trying to rescue his daughter from prostitution is the ageless country bumpkin unwittingly discovering the pleas-ures of sin in the city. The Spence Douthit who knows that his friend Floyd is guilty of murder and arson is wooden because, unlike great comic characters, he has not been created to re-spond to the tragic as well as the comic. At the end of *Tragic Ground*, Spence is extricated by his son-in-law from the des-perate life which has ruined Floyd, but the machinery of the rescue does not obscure the fact that Spence now looks more

35. *Georgia Boy* (New York: Grosset and Dunlap, 1943), p. 223.

like a monster than a clown. And the final question which he raises is not how to reform society, but how to transform human nature.

Caldwell's portrait of human nature, despite his insistence that he writes directly from observation, seems a caricature. The essential strokes are few: apathy, irresponsibility, amorality, defective intelligence, limited experience, and uninhibited sensuality. The life of people thus constituted is a brief thrashing about in a wasted country where violence relieves the dreariness. The mirror which Caldwell says that he holds up to human nature reflects not a representative selection of mankind but a private chamber of horrors. The serious intention is to convict landlords and factory owners of mutilating human life by warping its economic base. With decent wages and adequate shelter, then, these people presumably would grow clean, energetic, and conventionally well-behaved. Some of them do go off to town and prosper, but even these retain their old patterns. Jim Leslie, who lives on Augusta's Nob Hill, is as lecherous as his father Ty Ty. It is difficult to imagine Caldwell's characters having a past or future against which to measure any rise or fall. The degradation of the moment fills the foreground and obliterates the perspective, and the texture of time which complicates the work of Faulkner and Wolfe is absent. Change in the form of psychological or spiritual growth is not possible in these characters. Instead, their monotony of personality is an extension of the deadly tedium which surrounds them.

The victims of malnutrition, disease, debilitating climate, and boredom, these people are embedded in apathy and lethargy which would seem to belie the possibility of violent action. Clay Horey has never taken his syphilitic child to the doctor or even given the boy the medicine once bought. Pluto Swint, barrel-sized candidate for sheriff in *God's Little Acre*, sinks into the shade of a tree more often than he solicits votes. When the wife of Shep Barlow, whose daughter triggered the lynching in *Trouble in July*, drowned in the well, Shep found it easier to plug the well with household goods than to hoist the body out. The whites candidly recognize that Negro labor is essential to them. When Semon Dye shoots the Negro Hardy who tried to recover his wife from the preacher, Clay Horey worries that it is planting time, and he will have to go to work if Hardy dies. The crowd of lynchers in *Trouble in July* defends its method of keeping Negroes in order by hanging one occasionally instead of sending them out of the country as Narcissa Calhoun proposes. One of the men comments, "Hell, if there wasn't no more niggers in the country, I'd feel lost without them. . . . Besides, who'd do all the work, if the niggers was sent away?"[36]

A fatalistic acceptance of what is justifies sloth. "I was born poor," Spence Douthit informs the welfare worker, "and I'll die poor, and I won't be nothing but poor in between."[37] Caldwell makes clear that Spence, who was resigned to a life dependent upon charity, considered rebellion against this condition futile. He therefore has no sympathy for Floyd's protest by killing Bubber. Jeeter hands the Lesters' economic problems over to God to solve. Having provided land and sun and rain, He ought also to furnish seeds and fertilizer.

Despite the prevailing apathy among these people, there is inexhaustible sexual energy. It is the chief cause of violence and the center of the most extreme situations. The possibility that Spence is running after the pretty young social worker brings his wife screeching from her invalid's pallet. Throughout the novels fights break out as the men defend the females they possess. Clay Horey, for example, not only struggles with the preacher Semon Dye, but has to borrow a hundred dollars on next year's crop in order to regain title to his current wife. Buck Walden, Ty Ty's son, has trouble beating back the admirers of his wife Griselda. Fortunately, Ty Ty himself

36. *Trouble in July*, p. 191.
37. *Tragic Ground*, p. 21.

limits his attentions to verbal advertisements of Griselda's charms, but Buck has to shoot his brother Jim Leslie for poaching.

The classic case of violence in the South involving race relations and sexual taboos is, of course, lynching. Caldwell and Faulkner compound the horror by lynching innocent men, the white Lee Goodwin in *Sanctuary* and the Negro Sonny Clark in *Trouble in July*. In Caldwell's novel the lynching is preceded by wanton attacks on innocent Negroes under the pretense of trying to locate the suspect Sonny. Men break into Luke Bottomly's cabin and beat the Negro and pour turpentine over his wife. They terrify Amos Green's wife, who is alone, by catechizing her about how Negro rapists should be treated. Someone fires a chickenhouse, and while the crowd pauses to watch the flames, a few men sneak back to Amos Green's cabin. When the lynchers finally meet Sonny, they first blast away at the rabbit he has been carrying in his shirt. Caldwell has to give only the briefest account of the actual lynching because he has fully exploited its mood and manner in building up tension before the event.

The most violent coloring in Caldwell's fiction is extracted from sexual exploits. These occur as public performances. Perhaps Caldwell is remembering the publicity given to "family feuds, secreted births, mysterious deaths, violent quarrels, desertions, infidelities, and scandalous love-makings" in discussions at the cottonseed oil mill where he worked briefly as a boy.[38] By including one or more spectators in the story to comment on the activities or to converse amiably with the participants, Caldwell violates social convention in the direction of the grotesque. With pitchfork in hand, Semon Dye supervises the meeting of Clary Horey and Lorene in the barn loft. Spence Douthit chats genially with his daughter Libby and Jim Howard when he finds them in bed, licensed but unmarried. Will Thompson rips off Griselda's clothes in the presence of his wife, his sister-in-law, and Pluto Swint, and drags off his

38. *Call It Experience*, p. 15.

victim like a god—or a barbarian—mastering a not unwilling maiden. These public displays make another point for Caldwell. Privacy is a luxury unknown to the poor. They lack the dignity of being able to withdraw and be aware of their own individuality. The presence of witnesses reduces the possibly romantic private relations to gross physical contacts. When the shocks and surprises of these accumulate, they seem the attributes of a subhuman species to which violence is native. Occasionally Caldwell relieves the monotony of exploitative sex by introducing a kind of tenderness. Lov Bensey, who married Jeeter's daughter Pearl when she was twelve, has never been spoken to by his wife, but he has a bewildered dependence on her beauty. She herself wants only to escape from the tobacco road where no one ever laughs. Ty Ty defines sexual energy as God in man, but his simple identification is thwarted by the preachers who set up inhibitory rules which keep man in trouble.

Ty Ty seems to have in mind narrow morality of the sort which deems the refusal to dance, drink, smoke, or apply cosmetics the mark of a godly life. Such negativism, labeled "puritanism," has been blamed by critics like H. L. Mencken for the backwardness of the South. This kind of repressive religion has existed alongside the tradition of easy sociability in a tension which at its best reminds the Southerner of the difference between the demands of this world and the next, and which at its worst, misconstrues legalism for faith. Religion as mere restriction and proscription invites the violent parody which many writers have made of it. That passion for the spirit and passion for the flesh may be easily confused provides an anomalous violence which is simple to exploit.

Because in Caldwell's fiction trouble springs from the single dimension of caricature, its violence is a momentary disturbance rather than a permanent revelation of human nature or of the South. The people are cartoons and the social propaganda an elongated comic strip. Both the characters and the incidents are portrayed vigorously, but their created world is too contingent upon special circumstances to be convincing. The grotesque enlargement of a few traits is a literary method which bypasses the tragic implications of the comic for the sake of horror that is never resolved into pity.

3

Of the three writers considered here, William Faulkner employs violence and grotesqueness in the most complex way. His world, articulated as Yoknapatawpha County, Mississippi, is peopled by faded gentry, simple-minded farmers, impoverished merchants, and latter-day carpetbaggers; with idiots, criminals, and the insane. These submit to a fate which Faulkner has elaborated as his myth of the South, not a documentary report but his imagination's account of people so strongly rooted in one place that they are free to become symbols of universal human nature.

The lives of Faulkner's characters are never monotonous routines of boredom such as Caldwell portrays. Instead, they are freighted with destiny; the immediate act may be violent or perverse but it is part of a continuity too inclusive and too inexorable in its movement to be controlled by a single person. Characters have little choice in what happens to them. They are not presented anything so clear-cut as the head-heart division which Wolfe's young men struggle to reconcile. They may sense design in the universe, but their chief relationship to it is to be used by it, frequently in ways that involve frenetic quarrels, deadly fights, destruction of property, sexual violation, murder, suicide, and lynching. The human being fails the design in at least two ways: like Popeye he may be incapable of envisioning order and meaning and thus blindly stumbles through life, or like Thomas Sutpen he may be seduced by his own limited concept of the order which he wants to impose where the creative power of the universe intends some grander scheme. Human nature flawed in these ways is necessarily involved in disorder and disaster. Man, in addition to destroying himself out of his violence, wrecks the land, the natural surrogate of universal order. Although man is cast in a cataclysmic drama by power which he does not understand, he is judged in his role. The power of violence in Faulkner to a large extent lies in this fact. Faulkner keeps in tension the paradox that man is both determined and free. Man never knows the full meaning of his acts, but he is held responsible for their consequences. This view invests his violence with more complicated meaning than it has in the work of Wolfe and Caldwell.

One of Faulkner's characters impelled by fate is Joe Christmas in *Light in August* (1932). Anonymous from the time he is left at an orphanage on Christmas Eve, he spends himself in a search for a relationship which will identify him. He intuitively accepts the shadow of having Negro blood, a possibility confirmed only by his grandfather, Doc Hines, at the end of the novel. The first method of organizing his life which is offered him is the punishment-and-reward formula of the Calvinist McEacherns, who adopt the boy. It fails because Mrs. McEachern destroys the scheme with compassion. Joe can understand being beaten for failing to learn the catechism. Punishment requires merely that he endure, but sympathy demands a return from him. As long as he knows nothing about himself, however, he has nothing to give.

Having rejected the equation which the McEacherns offer, Joe drifts from violence to violence. In his thirty-third year he wanders to Jefferson, where his fate converges with that of Joanna Burden, Doc Hines, Gail Hightower, and, indirectly, Lena Grove. Among the first three he sets off the violence which their lives have anticipated. For Joanna Burden, spinster descendant of abolitionists, Joe is nemesis. He satisfies her bizarre sexual demands, but resists her plan that he become an acknowledged Negro. Obsessed by the feeling that something is going to happen to him, he cuts Miss Burden's throat. For

Doc Hines, Joe's arrest and jailing is an opportunity to incite the crowd to lynch his grandson as a sacrifice to Hines' religion of annihilating Negroes. For Gail Hightower, Joe himself seems to choose suicide when he escapes from his jailers only to run to Hightower's house where the young soldier Percy Grimm shoots him down and castrates him as he dies. At the moment of death, Joe's eyes contain an unfathomable knowledge. The violence of the white man releases Joe from the conflict of black and white which had immobilized him in life, but it settles on the whites a guilt which will remain "in whatever peaceful valleys, beside whatever placid and reassuring streams of old age, in the mirroring faces of whatever children they will contemplate old disasters and newer hopes."[39] It will prevent the accumulation of apathy which dulls the conscience. One part of the community then will not withdraw from the other in negligent complacency and refuse to suffer for or with its neighbor.

In contrast to the passivity of Joe Christmas which drifts into turbulence, the quietude of Lena Grove creates calm. Heavy with the child of the man who has deserted her, Lena walks from Alabama to Mississippi, stops in Jefferson to have her baby, and moves on to Tennessee. Her imperturbability and patience, which by implication are the redeeming virtues of people who live close to the earth, frame the violence of Joe Christmas' story and deaden its clangor. The tempo of her life moves to an inner measure; it neither hastens nor slackens under external pressures. This stability which is elemental and not self-conscious holds in place everything immediately around it. The isolation of Joe Christmas is impossible to Lena because she cannot even think of herself as cut off and alone. She eats and sleeps, moves and talks, and bears a child without raising a question about who she is. As the embodiment of female fertility she is in harmony with herself and the earth and thus is free from violence.

39. *Light in August* (Rahway, New Jersey: Quinn and Boden Co., Inc., 1932), p. 440.

Another of Faulkner's early novels, *As I Lay Dying* (1930), is populated by unreflective, accepting country folk like Lena Grove. Dr. Peabody believes that people like the Bundrens can be explained by the land; it, like the weather and the rivers, is overripe: "opaque, slow, violent; shaping and creating the life of man in its implacable and brooding image."[40] The doctor imaginatively makes a connection between meteorology and violence which can be partially verified. Crimes against persons increase in the summer and crimes against property in the winter. But whether there is a cause and effect relation between rising temperatures and exacerbated tempers which burst into violence has not been established. It is plausible, however, to consider the frustration of acute physical discomfort from heat and humidity a possible contributor, among other causes, to the high rate of murder and non-negligent manslaughter in the South. In 1959, for example, the national rate of 4.8 per 100,000 population was exceeded by all Southern states. This pattern prevails not only for homicide but also for aggravated assault, robbery, larceny, and auto theft.[41] Because the methods for formulating these statistics vary from state to state, comparisons cannot be strictly accurate; however, the figures for the South are so excessively high as to establish the fact that the people of this region account for more than their share of violence in the nation. Dr. Peabody's image of the river suggests to the reader that the sluggish flow of life through soporific heat may burst into floods of violence. In "Dry September" Faulkner brings the head-splitting heat into the story as an unnamed character which helps to press others into lynching Will Mayes. The Bundrens, matching their life with the land's, inch through the steamy, recently flooded country toward Jefferson, where they are determined to bury Addie.

Different from the Bundrens in her intensity, Addie lived by the blood, not by the brain which feels nothing and only

40. *The Sound and the Fury & As I Lay Dying* (New York: Modern Library, 1946), p. 369.
41. *Statistical Abstract of the United States, 1961*, p. 141.

receives words that have no real meaning. Like Wolfe's suicidal C. Green, she used violence to compel the attention of others. As a teacher, when she whipped a child until the blood ran from the welts, she thought, "Now you are aware of me!"[42] Anse Bundren's limited nature was no match for hers. She must live intensely because, as McCaslin Edmonds tells young Isaac McCaslin, "there is only one thing worse than not being alive, and that's shame."[43] Without shame she loved the preacher Whitfield and named her son by him Jewel. The fierceness of Addie's living so as "to get ready to stay dead a long time" seemed merely sinful pride to a conventionally pious women like Cora Tull. Addie welcomes the jeopardy as the risk which proves life. Lena Grove at the opposite pole needs to take no risks because she is elemental life. Between these two forms of energy are the Cora Tulls, respectable but not alive.

The series of accidents out of which Faulkner builds the funeral trip is a parade of human and natural disasters. At the river, where a flood has carried away the bridge, the wagon overturns, the mules drown, and Cash's leg is broken. As the days pass, the odor of the decomposing body increases and buzzards join the group. Cash's leg burns and blackens in its cement cast. At the Gillespies', Darl sets fire to the barn. Jewel helps to rescue the animals before he frees his mother's coffin, pushing it end over end out of the building. The stolid Bundrens have the same defense as Lena Grove. Violence washes to nothing against their impassiveness.

When the Bundrens at last reach Jefferson, they have to borrow shovels in order to dig the grave. They have fulfilled their obligation, but Faulkner has not exhausted their problems. Darl is arrested and sent to the asylum at Jackson. Dewey Dell is assaulted by the drugstore clerk from whom she had hoped to buy medicine to end her pregnancy. Only Anse gains by the trip. He slicks himself up, buys a set of teeth,

42. *The Sound and the Fury & As I Lay Dying*, p. 462.
43. "The Old People," *Go Down, Moses and Other Stories* (New York: Random House, 1942), p. 186.

and appears after the burial carrying the suitcase of the woman from whom he had borrowed the shovels. To his gaping family he says, "Meet Mrs. Bundren." The distance between the expected behavior and the actual behavior makes the occasion humorously grotesque. This conclusion discounts the preceding violence which points toward catastrophe. Instead, as Edwin Burgum observes, "What might have been a powerful sinister conclusion is almost reduced to the vaudeville level," the kind of reduction frequently practiced by Caldwell.[44] The fear and terror in the violence are drained out in the untouched naïveté of the participants.

Sanctuary (1931), called a pot-boiler by Faulkner, is simple in style and structure. Popeye, however, exemplifies the kind of character who becomes violent because he is so physically and psychologically inadequate as to be grotesque. His fate is more genetically determined than that of most Faulkner characters, but the information to support this conclusion is not related until the end of the novel. There the reader learns that Popeye is the mentally and sexually defective son of a syphilitic father. His criminal career, thus, is the signature of a predetermined failure; it is not an expression of swashbuckling freedom as racketeering is for the Great Gatsby.

The violence which surrounds Temple, daughter of Judge Drake, measures the corruption hidden in Temple's world and flagrant in Popeye's underworld. Popeye's crimes are physical and lurid: the corncob rape of Temple, her imprisonment in Miss Reba's brothel, the murder of Tommy, a henchman, and later the killing of Red, the lover provided for Temple. Popeye escapes punishment until on his way home for a summer visit he is arrested—in glaring irony—"for killing a man in one town and at an hour when he was in another town killing somebody else."[45] No one is interested in fixing testimony now, and Popeye, who refuses to defend himself, is hanged. Because Popeye is more a mechanical object than a person—

44. *The Novel and the World's Dilemma* (New York: Oxford University Press, 1947), p. 216.
45. *Sanctuary* (New York: Grossett and Dunlap, n.d.), p. 370.

"he had that vicious depthless quality of stamped tin"—his fate is less interesting in itself than as a test of those around him.[46]

Most of the upper-class whites fail the test and prove themselves more subtly corrupt than the outcasts. Horace Benbow, the lawyer for Lee Goodwin, Popeye's confederate falsely accused of raping Temple, is the only white Southerner who acts honorably, but his motives are doubted by the citizens of Jefferson and misunderstood by his family. The rest of the quality are corrupt both in their private lives and in their public offices. Gowan Stevens had been too drunk and cowardly to protect Temple. The District Attorney and Judge Drake buy Senator Clarence Snopes, who had helped Benbow locate Temple. With the approval of her elders, Temple, the one witness who could clear Goodwin, commits perjury. Aside from the melodramatic simplifications of plot and character, the violence asserts that aristocratic heroes and heroines are as capable of villainy as are villains. Heroism is still denied the white aristocrats when Faulkner completes the story of Temple Drake in *Requiem for a Nun* (1951). Here through violence a Negro makes expiation possible for Temple. By suffocating Temple's child, the maid shocks the white woman into admitting her guilt and complicity. In *Intruder in the Dust* (1948) Faulkner gives Lucas Beauchamp, the old Negro saved from lynching, a similar role as the conscience of Southern whites.

Violence precipitates around Joe Christmas and Popeye while they wait for things to happen, but disaster engulfs Thomas Sutpen when he tries to force destiny to take the shape of his plans. *Absalom, Absalom!* (1963) is the answer to the question which Sutpen asks only once: "You see, I had a design in mind. Whether it was a good or a bad design is beside the point; the question is, Where did I make the mistake in it, what did I do or misdo in it, whom or what injure by it to the extent which this would indicate."[47] *This* is

46. *Ibid.*, p. 2.
47. *Absalom, Absalom!* (New York: Modern Library, 1951), p. 263.

the debacle of his family, land, and fortune. The answer is tortuously threaded out by Faulkner over a time line which twists and turns and crosses back on itself, so that at no point along the way is the maze clear to the reader. The chief narrators are Miss Rosa Coldfield, Sutpen's sister-in-law, and Quentin Compson, aided by his Harvard roommate Shreve McCannon. The story has been handed down to Quentin from his father and his grandfather, who was Sutpen's only friend in Jefferson. In piecing together the history, Quentin struggles to understand his past, and the Canadian Shreve compiles a view of the South. They, like the reader, can form their conclusions only at the end of the novel when all the narrative lines have been connected and the violence has achieved its purpose.

Sutpen's design is "to have land and niggers and a fine house" like the Virginia Tidewater aristocrats whose servant turned him from the front door when he was a boy.[48] The desire is more than the ambition of an aggrieved ego; it is an obsession to do "not what he wanted to do but what he just had to do, had to do it whether he wanted to or not, because if he did not do it he knew that he could never live with himself for the rest of his life. . . ."[49] Faulkner speaks of Sutpen's loss of innocence, but Sutpen retains a grotesque kind of innocence which blinds him to the consequences of seeing things only in the perspective of his design. He takes and discards property and people as they are "adjunctive" to his plan. When, for example, he learns that his wife is part Negro, not Spanish as he had been led to believe, he feels justified in putting her aside because she was not "through no fault of her own, adjunctive or incremental to the design which I had in mind. . . ."[50] The violence of the novel is rooted in this moral obtuseness.

Sutpen has the egomaniacal pride of a Captain Ahab. Unlike the puling narcissistic heroes which Irving Malin iden-

48. *Ibid.*, p. 238.
49. *Ibid.*, p. 220.
50. *Ibid.*, p. 240.

tifies as characteristic of the Gothic strain in contemporary American fiction,[51] Sutpen can imagine how to externalize his pride and self-love in an estate and a dynasty, and he has the will and the energy to create what he imagines. When the Greek protagonist acts defiantly, he knows that he is defying the gods and fate, but Sutpen is puzzled by the recalcitrance of fate. He, like modern man, has never acknowledged the power of the mysterious. In his perverted selfhood, therefore, he wills violence and destruction.

Fate at first seems to allow Sutpen his design. In Jefferson he "tore violently," as Miss Rosa says, a plantation out of a hundred square miles of land wrested from a drunken Indian. He sired Henry and Judith to be his heirs. But a counter scheme of revenge enters when Sutpen's discarded wife sends their son Charles Bon to meet Henry at the university. Bon's engagement to Judith gives Sutpen two choices, either of which will destroy his design. He may recognize Bon as his son and thus acknowledge his first marriage, or he may remain quiet and let his daughter commit incest and miscegenation. Finally it is Henry who kills Bon.

The current of retribution and fatality, which Miss Rosa said Sutpen set moving, mounts into a flood of violence. Bon's son, Charles Etienne Saint Valery Bon, is brought to Jefferson, where he later lives with a full-blooded Negro wife and provokes a succession of wild fights, suffering like Joe Christmas from the conflict of black and white in him. Sutpen returns from the war determined to restore his land and house and to beget a new family. He takes the fifteen-year-old granddaughter of Wash Jones, his white handy man, but their child—a daughter—is worthless. Enraged by Sutpen's indifference, Wash kills Sutpen, the granddaughter, and the child. The design of Sutpen collapses utterly when Clytie fires the old home rather than relinquish Henry, who has come back there to die, to the care of Miss Rosa. The only remnant

51. See particularly the discussion of self-love in *New American Gothic* (Carbondale: Southern Illinois University Press, 1962).

of the House of Sutpen is Jim Bond, Charles Bon's idiot grandson, a wild creature occasionally seen dodging among the
ruins of the Hundred.

From this account of destruction with its Gothic details of
unacknowledged blood relationships, mysterious sources of
wealth, revenge, a midnight visit to a decaying mansion,
tangled wilds of forest and swamp, and atmosphere of gloom,
Shreve draws two conclusions: the Jim Bonds will eventually
conquer the Western world, becoming white in the process,
and Quentin hates the South, an emotion Quentin denies
hysterically. In Quentin's denial Faulkner seems to hate not
the consequences but the antecedent condition which destroyed the South: the egocentricism of man. Centered in his
own scheme for self-aggrandizement ("land and niggers and
a fine house"), man exploits natural and human resources. He
kills because nothing exists for him except as it is adjunctive to
his design. "Sutpen," Robert D. Jacobs comments, "is simply
the materialist who sets his rational will above the traditional
code of values (the old universals of love and honor and pity
and pride and sacrifice.")[52] Faulkner probes even deeper.
These universals were violated from the beginning by the nature of man. Sutpen was not an anomaly but an analogue for
the Southern white—for the American, for Everyman—who
glorifies self. The decay of the values is inevitable because
their health depends upon a sacramental treatment of the
whole of creation. This kind of respect is impossible so long as
man is centered in himself.

In *The Sound and the Fury* (1929) violence is the heat generated by the decay of the values which presumably the
Compson family once possessed. Economic and social failure
began with the Compson general "who put the first mortgage
on the still intact square mile to a New England carpetbagger
in '66, after the old town had been burned by the Federal Gen-

52. "Faulkner's Tragedy of Isolation," *Southern Renascence: The Literature of the Modern South*, ed. Louis D. Rubin, Jr., and Robert D. Jacobs
(Baltimore: The Johns Hopkins Press, 1963), p. 190.

eral Smith. . . ."[53] Faulkner takes up the moral disintegration
of the family in the seventh generation: Quentin III, Candace
(Caddy), Jason IV, and Benjamin. The time of the narrative
is Easter week end, 1928, the point from which the narrators
range back and forth through Compson history. Their violence is a dirge for the passing of integrity in a family which
is a microcosm of the South, of the community of man.

In the South, of course, the family has had a central position. The individualism fostered by the frontier and the plantation gave its allegiance to the family, which counted "connections" from early grandparents to remote cousins. The
honor of the family was identified with that of the person and
was just as promptly defended. The duello was the formal
embodiment of violence for the redress of insult or injury. If
among mountaineers the violence of feuds often outlasted the
memory of the cause, among aristocrats the duel became a
punctilio. In "An Odor of Verbena," one of the stories of the
Sartoris family, the mindless action of Bayard Sartoris, who
presents himself as a target, parodies the code. Not only may
the traditions of the family set off violence, but from a purely
literary standpoint the Southern family with its many kinds
of personalities and manners, occupations and incomes, per-
suasions and beliefs provides the writer a world in miniature.
And it is a world which preserves the past in talk. Robert N.
Linscott reports Faulkner as having said in effect, "Why, when
I was a little boy, there'd be sometimes twenty or thirty people
in the house, mostly relatives, aunts, uncles, cousins and
second cousins, some maybe coming for overnight and staying
on for months, swapping stories about the family and about
the past, while I sat in a corner and listened. That's where I
got my books."[54]

In writing about the Compsons, Faulkner treats the final
decline of the past. Section I of *The Sound and the Fury*, told

---

53. *The Sound and the Fury*, p. 7.
54. "Faulkner Without Fanfare," *Esquire*, LX (July, 1963), 38.

from Benjy's idiot mind, achieves a Joycean simultaneity of time in which the whole collapse of the family is set forth but without the chronology and interpretation which a sane mind needs to give meaning to experience. Benjy's fumbling thoughts circle around his two loves—Caddy and the pasture which is the last of the Compson Domain. The only way that Benjy can mourn the loss of these symbols of the family's honor and security is to blubber and howl.

Quentin, dominating Section II, chooses to mourn by committing suicide. He cannot live with the knowledge that Caddy, his ideal of chastity and honor, sets no value on herself and is doomed to promiscuity. In his desire to preserve Caddy intact he tries three violent actions which fizzle into melodramatic gestures; his family is no longer capable of producing a son with a genuinely heroic will. No one takes Quentin seriously. Caddy shrugs off his knife when he wants to kill her and himself. Dalton Ames, Caddy's lover, refuses to fight. Quentin imagines telling his father that he and Caddy have committed incest, thus gaining in his thought an eternal punishment in hell: *"the clean flame the two of us more than dead. Then you will have only me then only me then the two of us amid the pointing and the horror beyond the clean flame."*[55] Without physical or moral vitality Quentin is powerless to act for the values he respects. His hypersensitivity in the end ruins the good he desires. Caddy is not worth despair, but two months after her marriage to a liar and cheat, Quentin drowns himself.

Jason, accounted a sane Compson, is mad with frustration. His section of the novel boils with the rage of a man doomed to petty business in Jefferson because Caddy's husband failed to give him a job in a bank as promised. The only point of calm is Dilsey, the old Negro cook, whose final division of the book completes the story of Jason's fury. At home Jason is goaded by the whining of his mother, the helplessness of Benjy, the

55. *The Sound and the Fury,* p. 135.

rebellion of Quentin, Caddy's daughter left to be brought up in Jefferson. The cynicism of Jason's father toward supporting a family which includes "shiftless niggers," a ne'er-do-well brother-in-law, and an idiot son has become scorn in Jason, who comments to his employer at the store:

I haven't got much pride, I can't afford it with a kitchen full of niggers to feed and robbing the state asylum of its star freshman. Blood, I says, governors and generals. It's a damn good thing we never had any kings and presidents: we'd all be down there at Jackson chasing butterflies.[56]

Nor has Jason any romantic illusions about honor and love and justice. In the end, however, he is as effectively betrayed by his lack of principle as Quentin was by an exaggerated sense of honor.

The ugliness of the Compsons' family life like that of the Gants' is expressed in violence. The hatred between Jason and Caddy's Quentin flares in bickering, quarreling, and physical violence when Jason tries to whip the seventeen-year-old girl. When Quentin runs away, taking nearly seven thousand dollars which Jason had hidden in his bedroom, he is reduced to inexpressible rage. Realizing that it is futile to hunt for Quentin, he gives up the chase and returns to Jefferson and a life in which loss and evil will be so constant that they will not seem like threats.

The only order is in the enduring Dilsey. In addition to the virtues of patience and fortitude, she has charity. She can answer the petulant calls of Mrs. Compson and withstand the wrath of Jason without losing her concern for the well-being of the Compsons. To her elemental willingness to accept circumstances, which she shares with characters like Lena Grove and the Bundrens, Faulkner had added the capacity to meet selfishness, anger, and hatred with love. This is the power by which Dilsey can support order against violence.

Faulkner, like Caldwell, uses violence to examine society,

56. *Ibid.*, p. 247.

but in an analysis more subtle than Caldwell's because it penetrates beyond the immediate maladjustment. It has been said that Faulkner rejects the modern South because it has traduced the honorable aristocratic code of the Old South.[57] But in Faulkner's view the code itself was tainted from the beginning. In the South slavery and in the North industry which fattened on slave-produced cotton were outward signs of the inner fall of man who always perverts the freedom which his Creator provided. Even when given a New World, including "a South for which He had done so much with woods for game and streams for fish and deep rich soil for seed and lush springs to sprout it and long summers to mature it and serene falls to harvest it and short mild winters for men and animals,"[58] he again lost Paradise. He carries into every beginning the configuration of the end, his lustful, proud, gluttonous self. That this corrupted nature sows and reaps little except destruction is abundantly dramatized in Faulkner's work.

Much of what passes for progress in the South offends Faulkner. The Snopeses, for example, rise to the top because their conniving and cheating are blessed as competition and rewarded in a cash-profit economy. Ike McCaslin in "The Bear" stories is Faulkner's chief spokesman against the spoilage of the land by paved highways, factories, and mechanized farms. Old Uncle Ike on his last hunting trip thinks about the destruction which man's misuse of the land has wrought:

This Delta. *This land which man has deswamped and denuded and derivered in two generations so that white men can own plantations and ride in jim crow cars to Chicago to live in millionaires' mansions on Lakeshore Drive, where white men rent farms and live like niggers and niggers crop in shares and live like animals, where cotton is planted and grows man-tall in the very cracks of the sidewalks, and usury and mortgage and bankruptcy and measureless wealth, Chinese and African and Aryan and*

57. See especially Maxwell Geismar, *Writers in Crisis: The American Novel Between Two Wars* (Boston: Houghton Mifflin Company, 1942); Malcolm Cowley, "William Faulkner's Legend of the South," *Sewanee Review*, LIII (July, 1945), 343-361; and Malcolm Cowley, "Introduction," *The Portable Faulkner* (New York: Viking Press, 1946).

58. "The Bear," *Go Down, Moses*, p. 283.

*Jew, all breed and spawn together until no man has time to say
which one is which nor cares.* . . . No wonder the ruined woods I
used to know don't care for retribution. . . . The people who have
destroyed it will accomplish its revenge.[59]

Hunting for Faulkner, like bullfighting for Hemingway, is
a ritual, an art, whereby violence and death are stylized and
given meaning. It is the form which contains man and nature
in a just relationship. The buck runs and the dogs chase
because that "was what they done the best and was proudest
at," and the hunters follow, testing their woodsmanship so that
they "would have the right to come back here next November. . . ."[60] But the relation of man to nature and of man to man
has been violated, and violence is an expression of this outrage.

Although violence and grotesqueness in Faulkner's work
are generally related to the dark side of man, these elements
also appear when Faulkner is being humorous. The roistering
exuberance of Southwest humor permeates the stories of the
Snopeses, the tribe of weevil-like whites whose invasion of the
middle class in Yoknapatawpha Faulkner began to detail in
The Hamlet (1940). To portray their advance he uses exaggeration, matter-of-fact reporting of the preposterous, ludicrous incongruity, and latent cruelty in the tradition of writers
like A. B. Longstreet, J. G. Baldwin, and George W. Harris,
and, later, Mark Twain. The rascality of men like Simon
Suggs, skilled in gulling the simple, reappears in Flem Snopes.
Flem, however, is more devious than his frontier counterparts, for he wants status and privilege for himself and the innumerable relatives who follow his trail. The son of barnburner Ab Snopes, Flem looks like a rural gargoyle:

. . . a thick squat soft man of no establishable age between
twenty and thirty, with a broad still face containing a tight seam
of mouth stained slightly at the corners with tobacco, and eyes
the color of stagnant water, and projecting from among the other

---

59. "Delta Autumn," *Go Down, Moses,* p. 364.
60. "Race at Morning," *Big Woods* (New York: Random House, 1955),
p. 188.

features in startling and sudden paradox, a tiny predatory nose like the beak of a small hawk.[61]

By a literal-minded, deadly serious discharge of his duties he comes up from the farm to clerk in Will Varner's store, to marry Varner's daughter Eula, to live on the Old Frenchman place, and finally to move on to Jefferson, a richer field for his talents.

Unlike a noisy frontiersman, Flem does not draw attention to himself by violent behavior; he is a catalyst stirring up others and remaining unchanged himself, except to pocket whatever profit comes from the turbulence. He turns the countryside topsy-turvy with spotted Texas ponies, but there is no proof that he profited from the sale of the wild animals. His greatest triumph is to trick Odum Bookwright, Henry Armstid, and U. K. Ratliff, the sewing machine salesman heretofore impervious to Snopes, into buying the Old Frenchman place, where they dig for buried treasure after finding the three bags of coins which Flem had judiciously planted there. Flem's self-effacement is skilful understatement by Faulkner; however, it is set against episodes of gross overstatement. The idiot boy Ike Snopes loves Jack Houston's cow, a grotesque relationship which Faulkner describes in the lushly poetic language of a summer idyl. Later Mink Snopes kills Houston, who has won the right to impound Mink's cattle until their pasturage is paid. After the murder, Mink drives his wife and children from home and devotes his nights to the labors of a haunted man. He fights off the hound that howls over the corpse, he dumps Houston's body into a hollow tree, he later exhumes the decayed mass and throws it into the river. When he returns to the tree to find the arm which had been torn off the body, he is caught by the sheriff.

In each episode there are other Snopeses eager to make money from the misery of their kinsmen. The evolution of these people is based on a principle of economic selection which violates all the efforts of man to civilize himself through

61. *The Hamlet* (New York: Random House, 1940), p. 52.

love, honor, and charity. Faulkner, however, keeps the balance between the comic and the grotesque more successfully than does Caldwell and thus succeeds in making Snopery a valid criticism of the nature of man and his society. The outrages perpetrated by the Snopeses are further chronicled in *The Town* (1957) and *The Mansion* (1959). In these Faulkner continues to invent raucous violence which in the midst of the uproar nonetheless exposes envy, greed, and lust.

At the root of violence in Faulkner lies his theme of man weak by nature and buffeted by fate. In Yoknapatawpha County, fate is the consequence—economic, social, and moral—of slavery and the war it necessitated, of the rape of the land both by farmers and by industrialists, and of the substitution of illusions about the past for integrity in the present. The intensity of the violence is a gauge of the horror Faulkner feels for human corruption, decay, and degeneration. These ideas continued to motivate his work as he experimented with new statements of them in the short stories in *Knight's Gambit* (1949) and in the novel *A Fable* (1954) with its Christian analogues.

The effect of violence and grotesqueness in the work of Wolfe, Caldwell, and Faulkner has been to de-romanticize the South, at least to the extent of destroying the myth of agrarian perfection. Among them they question the aristocratic tradition; they dispute racial purity by openly recognizing that miscegenation occurs; they portray the discontent of the poor; and they admit the presence of ignorance, indolence, and disease. They use violence to point up the difference between what they see and what fiction in the sentimental tradition has generally assumed about the South. Their work, as Willard Thorp concludes, is a defense of the region by acknowledging its shortcomings.[62]

In varying degrees these writers are sensitive to their region as the area where industrialism and urbanization are disrupt-

62. *American Writing in the Twentieth Century* (Cambridge: Harvard University Press, 1960), p. 237.

ing the social patterns which have remained undisturbed longer than those in any other section of the country. Neither the decline of the old order nor the emergence of the new is cause for optimism. For Caldwell, violence and more particularly grotesqueness are the very nature of the life of people who are automata, presumably reduced to that level by the economy. For Faulkner, violence inheres in the fate of man who bears the guilt of the past, when the dream of Eden was destroyed by slavery both on Southern farms and in Northern factories. For Wolfe, the dream died in the ugly disorder of small-town life, violent with the frustration and dishonesty that reflect man's irrationality.

Caldwell is the only one of the three writers who has made the grotesque a method of composition. Faulkner and Wolfe introduce the grotesque as subject matter expressing the distortion of personality or behavior which they wish to convey. The violence of language in Caldwell is dictated by the mindlessness of his characters, their illiteracy and their coarseness. Except for dialogue, Caldwell writes simply and matter-of-factly. Wolfe, on the other hand, creates the effect of violence by rhetorical devices such as massed epithets, invective, rapidly rising and falling cadences, exclamations, and words connoting extraordinary vigor and action.

In Faulkner the language expresses violence in complicated syntax. Words pass back and forth across the same area of thought or action until they are magnetized and attract to themselves every possible emotion and interpretation. Their movement around fixed points from which Faulkner contemplates events serves actually to temper the violence by reporting onstage the action which occurs offstage. This classical device allows the receiver to embellish the report out of his own imagination of evil. At the same time, the distance between the event and the reader prevents the action from overwhelming him. Alfred Kazin acutely notes that by reporting the acts of Joe Christmas, Faulkner not only has established the alienation of Christmas but also has created a stillness, "that depth of meditation into which all the characters are plunged."[63] The responses of the narrator interest Faulkner more than the activity, hence the experiments with multiple points of view in *The Sound and the Fury* and with the garrulous, philosophizing narrator in *Absalom, Absalom!* and *Requiem for a Nun*. The counterplay of several narrating voices telling the same violence makes important not the incident but the way in which it is seen. The teller who is enamored of words can subdue violence by examining and discussing it. The suspension of the event while the narrator ranges freely in time sets an undertow against the violence. In his subtle control and variation of language Faulkner portrays violence more vitally than do Wolfe and Caldwell.

Violence as an expression of the meaning of life is central in Faulkner and Caldwell but somewhat tangential in Wolfe. Wolfe embraced all experience so enthusiastically that he could look on violence with confidence also. Caldwell simplifies life with violence and grotesqueness until it has no dignity or significance beyond an instinctive holding on from moment to moment for food or sex. The opposite effect is achieved by Faulkner when violence and distortion prove how much man can endure for the sake of discovering that his spirit is indestructible.

63. "The Stillness of *Light in August*," *Twelve Original Essays on Great American Novels*, ed. Charles Shapiro (Detroit: Wayne State University Press, 1958), p. 267.

Part Two

Since 1940 a new generation of Southern writers has appeared. In the fiction of eight of these the use of violence has been consistently serious in conception and execution. This group by no means constitutes a "school." The authors are Southern by birth and upbringing, and several have continued to live in or near their original homes. They write about Southern people in Southern settings; the region is palpably present in their work. But they see individually.

Thus violence appears in many guises as it elucidates theme, intensifies mood, and delineates character. Out of the variety certain general achievements emerge. The violence gives aesthetic value to the incongruous, the ugly, the repulsive, and the chaotic which these sensitive observers see in their world. It expresses the suffering of inarticulate and dispossessed persons. It questions an optimistic faith in progress and human self-sufficiency by asserting the darkness in the heart of man. It protests that without some formal ordering of his experience man will be overwhelmed by the accidental and the relative. By expressing in the mode of violence the destructive forces in society and in human nature, these Southerners affirm their sense of order through the very disorder which violates it.

These contemporary Southern writers, like their predecessors, have brought exceptional literary talent to their work. Their ear for language includes the rhythms of expository and narrative prose as well as the intonations peculiar to each variety of colloquial Southern speech. They invent symbols and metaphors which participate in the total meaning. In creating character they combine the external authenticity of person in the nineteenth-century tradition of characterization with the internal validity of self-consciousness as taught by

Freud and Joyce. Their handling of time is complex because for them the history of the past and the individual in the present have never been separated. They enrich the texture of their stories and novels with tangible details of place. These give to the evocation of mood a solidity which is often absent from modern fiction. In their strong sense of the immediate they have the essential quality of story-telling: the narratives begin in the local and project into the universal, an extension which, after all, is our reason for reading fiction.

I. Violence and the integrity of the self: Robert Penn Warren

The senior member of the group of younger Southern writers of fiction who came to prominence after Wolfe's death and after Caldwell and Faulkner had completed several major works is Robert Penn Warren. His accomplishments and seniority make him today one of the most noted members of this group. Born in Guthrie, Kentucky, in 1905, Warren is only two years younger than Caldwell; but during the thirties when Caldwell was publishing novels like *Tobacco Road* and *God's Little Acre*, Warren was absorbed in writing poetry. While an undergraduate at Vanderbilt University he was a contributor to *The Fugitive*. Warren has continued to publish poems, but since the appearance of his first novel, *Night Rider*, in 1939, the bulk of his creative writing has been fiction: *At Heaven's Gate* (1943), *All the King's Men* (1946), *World Enough and Time* (1950), *Band of Angels* (1955), *The Cave* (1959), *Wilderness* (1961), and *Flood* (1964). A novelette, *Blackberry Winter*, appeared in 1946 and a collection of short stories, *The Circus in the Attic and Other Stories*, in 1947. As a distinguished editor and critic Warren has encouraged the publication of new American writers, including Eudora Welty, and has helped to develop the tenets of New Criticism.

As a writer of fiction Warren engages his characters in a single question: Who am I? Their search for identity directs the course of the plot. The thrust of the question into the consciousness of the characters and into circumstances provokes violence. As long as the character remains divided, a non-self, he is subject to violence either because he acts without direction or because he cannot act at all and thus becomes a pawn to the hysterical impulses of the crowd. Out of his action or, it may be, his passivity, he gains some degree of knowledge about himself. The mark of the effectiveness of this knowledge is the resolution of violence into a constructive pattern of life.

The ground for violence in Warren's novels is his conception of the nature of man. His view springs from traditional religious thought which accounts man a fallen creature. In emphasizing the depravity of man, Warren reflects the sturdy strain of Calvinism which permeated Protestantism in the South. He has grasped accurately the seriousness with which this concept informs Southern life, a seriousness which H. L. Mencken in blasting "puritanism" dismissed as superstition. Man, Warren asserts in his long narrative poem *Brother to Dragons*, is radically evil, irrational, and morally ambivalent. The soul is

> ... that hell-broth of paradox and internecine
> Complex of motive and murderous intensity.

Therefore,

> ... the origin of no human action,
> No matter how sweet the action and dear, is ever
> Pure like the flower.[1]

This imperfect, incomplete, chaotic being is set down in a world over which he has no control; things merely happen

1. *Brother to Dragons: A Tale in Verse and Voices* (New York: Random House, 1953), p. 56.

without apparent purpose. Having established his characters as wicked by nature, Warren does not then offer them a religious scheme of redemption. Instead he explores the psychological manifestation of this corruption, the inability to form a clear image of the self. The action symbolic of the division within Warren's characters is their rejection of their fathers. This denial inevitably disorders their lives and plunges them into violence. Rejection is followed by flight either toward a father substitute, who then proves to be false and betrays his protégé, or simply away from the intolerable confusion created by the unknown self toward some vision of peace. The return of a character to his childhood home or to his father with love and acceptance, therefore, signifies both his reconciliation with the image of himself contained in the father as a representative of the past, and an essential step toward a mature integration of the self in the present. It is only on this basis, Warren implies, that man can achieve order either in his own personality or in his society. Not all of the chief characters complete the full cycle of growth from the knowledge of evil to reconciliation with the past and acceptance of responsibility for the present. But when they do so, Warren most successfully dramatizes the meaning of violence in his work. This achievement distinguishes *All the King's Men,* for here he traces the complete psychological pattern of rejection, flight, and return.

The way to self-knowledge lies through violence, pain, and suffering. Only an affirmation of all that is frightening about human life leads to truth,

> For whatever hope we have is not by repudiation,
> And whatever health we have is not by denial,
> But in confronting the terror of our condition.
> All else is a lie.[2]

"The terror of our condition" is the thematic core of Warren's fiction, and nothing short of violence could be a genuine revelation of the tension between good and evil, ideal and actu-

2. *Ibid.,* p. 192.

ality, order and disorder, the self and the non-self which strains man's life. In treating these polarities Warren fills the foreground with violence so that he not only exposes the flaws of human nature but also illuminates whatever capacity for achieving integrity man possesses. Because Warren delineates in the fullest detail that stage of the development which is the chaos between rejection and acceptance, readers are likely to be impressed by the quantity of the violence rather than its purpose.

In the plots of the novels Warren repeatedly portrays the psychological dissociation of the individual. It is for this purpose that he dramatizes social, political, and economic problems from the history of the South. These constitute explosive, inherently violent situations. The destructive violence of man's nature is made graphic by the action which historical events provide in the narrative. From Southern history Warren has chosen incidents of violence: in *World Enough and Time* he uses the Beauchamp tragedy of 1825 and the conflict between Relief and Anti-Relief factions in Kentucky politics; in *Band of Angels,* the problems of a young mulatto woman before and after the Civil War; in *Night Rider,* the warfare between tobacco farmers and buyers in Kentucky early in the twentieth century; in *At Heaven's Gate,* the career of Tennessee speculator Luke Lea; in *The Cave,* the death of Floyd Collins; in *Flood,* the inundation of a small Tennesse town following the construction of a dam; and in *All the King's Men,* the rise and fall of Huey Long. Recently he returned to the Civil War, setting *Wilderness* against the second Wilderness campaign. As Charles R. Anderson points out, however, "Warren always makes it clear that he is concerned with the unchanging nature of man rather than with the changing social fabric in which this nature manifests itself."[3] Specifically, Warren is concerned with the possibility of change in the nature of man so that it becomes responsive rather than apathetic, gen-

3. "Violence and Order in the Novels of Robert Penn Warren," *Southern Renascence,* p. 210.

erous rather than selfish, orderly rather than chaotic. In each
novel he combines the inner violence of major characters with
the overt violence of the historical germ of the story to create
various perspectives on the relation of violence to the meaning
of man's life.

In examining problems of economic and social justice,
Warren shows that systems of human organization go awry
because individuals fail. Some persons like Percy Munn, the
young lawyer in *Night Rider,* are so incapacitated by a lack
of identity by which to keep order within themselves that they
cannot maintain the order of an external system; others like
Bogan Murdock, the speculator in *At Heaven's Gate,* subscribe to totalitarian methods of imposing a false order. Mr.
Munn joins the tobacco farmers and leads them with the intention of securing justice against the buyers' monopoly. A cold
and empty man, Munn hunts for a definition of himself
through a relation with another person or through an act on his
part, but Warren dooms him in both respects because without
a self Munn cannot be genuinely related to others nor can he
act decisively. The isolation of Munn is signified in part by the
author's referring to him as "Mr. Munn," as though the title
is a public dignity to mask the private hollowness. Munn can
admire but cannot emulate persons who have achieved the
equilibrium of knowing themselves. The only quiet in his life
comes from his perception of that quality in others. Captain
Todd, an aging Confederate veteran who serves on the board
of the association of tobacco growers, impresses him with "his
calmness, what appeared to be his deep, inner certainty of
self, his caution and detachment and tolerance in regard to the
world outside himself."[4] Such integrity Munn believes can be
secured only by living through a testing experience staunchly
enough "to come out on the other side of it afterward and still
be yourself."[5] This capacity is exactly what Munn lacks, hence

4. *Night Rider* (Boston: Houghton Mifflin Company, 1939), p. 43.
5. *Ibid.*

he brings chaos and destruction to others and suicide to himself.

The logical extension of a psychological disorientation like Percy Munn's is a ruthless, inhuman personality which exploits others. Such a person is Bogan Murdock, Warren's portrait of the non-self who inflicts economic ruin. He is especially loathsome in a democratic society because he buys and sells the machinery of democracy. Legislators vote away the resources of the state at his direction. Hirelings break a strike against his lumber company. Innocent men are ruined by his falsification of collateral on state bank deposits. Murdock is Warren's most severe comment on the collapse of values in a competitive urban organization which has turned human beings into ciphers of profit and loss. The empire which he establishes is a false order because its creator is false. He has no knowledge of himself to which he can be true. Without this guide he can produce only violence and disaster.

Munn, isolated from others by his lack of self-knowledge, is capable of murder and arson. He is chosen to lead the raid which ends in the murder of Trevelyan, a recalcitrant member of the protective society who tried to blackmail one of the night riders. Before Trevelyan is killed, only Munn removes his mask—"its privacy was hideous"—but Munn's isolation is so complete that he is not even sure his bullet hit Trevelyan. Munn again leads when the night riders dynamite tobacco warehouses and blow up the bridge to French Springs. At the mention of the possibility of mining the bridge to explode when troops are crossing the structure, he is aware of how easily violence has become his way of living. He automatically notes that there would be good cover for attacking the bridge: "It got so a man's mind ran that way."[6] In this vein Irene Hendry concludes that Munn represents "the nineteenth-century philosophic man in the process of becoming, through violence in combination with organization, the twentieth-

6. *Ibid.*, p. 304.

century political man." Lacking a real self, he becomes "the soldier of a modern mechanized army or the citizen of a totalitarian state."[7]

Another violent consequence of the deadly coldness of the man who has no identity is his violation of the trust and happiness of persons close to him. Munn realizes that to his wife he predicts disaster for the tobacco association because "he wanted . . . to deepen that look of concern on her face, to frighten her, to make her aware of the evil and the instability in the world, to make her suffer."[8] After the murder of Trevelyan, Munn forces his wife so crudely that she leaves him. He next seduces Lucille, a friend's daughter. Her father, shocked by the betrayal, dies. Lucille tells Munn, "Whatever you did, you were cold."[9] The parallels between public and private violence are not this neatly drawn by Warren in other novels, but the movement from the unfeeling non-self to the violation of others often occurs. In *All the King's Men*, for example, Jack Burden pushes Anne Stanton toward destruction by ignoring her legitimate claims on him for love and friendship. Brad Tolliver of *Flood* provokes adultery and murder by flaunting his sexual success. Bogan Murdock tyrannizes over his family until his wife is driven to alcoholism and his daughter to a rebellion which leads eventually to her murder.

This rebellion is part of a movement of rejection and reconciliation between father and child which appears first in *At Heaven's Gate*. The cycle recurs in each of the succeeding novels as the symbol of man's discovery of the self. It gains complexity when Warren associates the father with history. Although essential to the integrity of the self, the passage from rejection to reconciliation is never easy. The child always risks being devoured by the parent. "It is the blood greed, and it is the fate of a man," Jack Burden recognizes.[10] In *At*

7. "The Regional Novel: The Example of Robert Penn Warren," *Sewanee Review*, LIII (Jan., 1945), 101.
8. *Night Rider*, p. 127.
9. *Ibid.*, p. 441.
10. *All the King's Men* (New York: Harcourt, Brace and Company, 1946), p. 39.

Heaven's Gate the violence which overtakes the young people is in proportion to the vehemence of their rejection of the father. Sue Murdock rejects her father because he considers her another piece of his property to be made to perform according to his wishes. Although her behavior in the group of young Bohemians which she joins is as promiscuous as Caddy Compson's in *The Sound and the Fury*, Sue does not crave annihilation but identity through a man who is real, a pursuit, however, which is still a flight from herself. Another member of the coterie, the poet Slim Sarrett, has rejected his father in order to fashion a past more in keeping with the demands of his imagination. Of the group Sarrett is the most seriously disordered by his divided nature; he is a liar and a homosexual. Intellectually he perceives that "the tragic flaw in the Shakespearean hero is a defect in self-knowledge," but emotionally he is unable to cope with the self he does not acknowledge and is betrayed by it into violence.[11] Blinded by self-pity, he strangles Sue because "she shouldn't laugh at him."[12] Jerry Calhoun, Sue Murdock's fiancé, rejects his inept, countrified father in order to fashion himself in the image of the urbane Murdock. After Murdock's dishonesty has been exposed, Jerry returns home to face the violence which he has carried in his heart. Rejecting his father and aunt and uncle, he realizes, had been tantamount to murdering them. This recognition may lead Jerry to accept his family and his past, but Warren does not complete the cycle; he simply ends the novel. The one of the four young people who is least affected by violence is Sweetwater, presumably because he has achieved at least a partial reconciliation with his father.

In subsequent novels Warren combines in a single character the two manifestations of an inadequate definition of the self which in his first two novels he keeps separate: the exploitation of others because of an inability to consider them human, and the denial of the claims of the past as represented

11. *At Heaven's Gate* (New York: Harcourt, Brace and Company, 1943), p. 196.
12. *Ibid.*, p. 362.

by the father. Furthermore he treats the violation of others as part of the problem of converting an idea into action. These developments deepen and complicate his portrayal of violence.

Rejection of the father in *All the King's Men* is a central motif more substantially related to the problem of violence and self-knowledge than it is in any other of Warren's novels. Jack Burden bears a name which connotes the load of guilt carried by the isolated, disoriented self. An alert young reporter academically trained in history, Jack is the modern compartmentalized man who assumes that there is no relation between what he thinks and what he does, that his vocation is merely a job, that a detached spectator can never be involved in violence. Warren has liberally supplied him with fathers: Ellis Burden, the attorney presumed to be his real father; Judge Irwin, his lifelong friend and mentor; Governor Stanton, the father of his two closest friends Anne and Adam; and finally, Willie Stark, the ambiguous politician on whose staff he serves. One by one he finds reasons for discarding these men. At last he precipitates the death of Irwin by confronting him with the facts of his collusion with Governor Stanton years before which had brought to suicide Mortimer Littlepaugh, the man ruined by their action. When Irwin commits suicide, Mrs. Burden reveals that he was Jack's father. For the first time Jack is shocked into recognizing his complicity in all the violence which had touched him. In meditating on the circle of violence in which "Mortimer had killed Judge Irwin because Judge Irwin had killed him, and I had killed Judge Irwin because Judge Irwin had created me," he comes to the conclusion that "the truth always kills the father, the good and weak one or the bad and strong one, and you are left alone with yourself and the truth. . . ."[13]

The discovery of his real father reverses Jack's relation to Willie. He returns to his job, but he withdraws from the power struggle between Stark and his political rival MacMur-

13. *All the King's Men*, pp. 374-375.

fee. The penalty for rejecting his father and for taking as a substitute the wrong man—Willie—had been disaster for those around him and near destruction for himself. He had accepted the dictum of his sterile world that a detached mind and an unengaged heart were the virtues of civilization. Having been further instructed by Willie that "there is always something" by which to catch up another, he had come close to believing that at the least he could choose whether or not to play the game and that at the most the game had no meaning. But his choice had brought him only to violence. The catastrophe, however, does not destroy Jack; it forces him to acknowledge his relation to the past and to accept his responsibility to the present.

In the concluding pages of the novel he sorts out the meaning of violence to his life. By the theory of historical costs or the moral neutrality of history, he had previously explained to himself that only results, not the process, can be judged, that violence is the price of change, that "maybe a man has to sell his soul to get the power to do good."[14] When he realizes that the invitation of the henchman Duffy to work for him implies a complicity in all the evil of Willie's career, Jack sees himself as much a conspirator against life and order as any of Willie's "boys" had been. At this stage he hates himself and Willie. He stays away from his home town and from Anne, reminders of his past. The crisis during this period of reaction is his impulse to incite Sugar-Boy to kill Duffy in order to take revenge for Duffy's having set Adam to assassinate Willie. But the image of Duffy winking at him in fraternal collusion restrains him.

In the third stage of his contemplation he calls on Lucy Stark. She believes that Willie was a great man. Eventually Jack comes to agree: "And believing that Willie Stark was a great man, I could think better of all other people, and of myself."[15] By accepting his mother and stepfather as genuine

14. *Ibid.*, p. 418.
15. *Ibid.*, p. 452.

people and by returning to Anne Stanton, Jack changes from a neutral spectator to a concerned participant. He has to live through the violence of demagoguery, suicide, and murder before he understands that his involvement carries the same kind of responsibility which Cass Mastern, the great-uncle whose biography he is writing, had recognized when he admitted "that all of these things—the death of my friend, the betrayal of Phebe, the suffering and rage and great change of the woman I had loved—all had come from my single act of sin and perfidy, as the boughs from the bole and the leaves from the bough."[16] Once Jack is willing to be responsible for the consequences of the evil and violence which he even unknowingly generates, then, as John L. Stewart observes, "he emerges from the womblike state of abstract knowledge without responsibility which, like Stark's abstract power and Stanton's abstract science, withholds men from full participation in life."[17] He will finish his book, a kind of settlement with the past, and he and Anne will leave Burden's Landing to go "into the convulsion of the world, out of history into history and the awful responsibility of Time."[18]

The statement of responsibility in this novel is Warren's fullest answer in fiction to the problem of violence. The man of self-knowledge is characterized by a mature acceptance of the strengths and weaknesses of his father and, consequently, of the past. He is prepared to act free from the most serious errors of ignorance, delusion, and immaturity. He and his action will not be faultless, for the nature of man contains the unfathomable, but the integrated, responsible self is unlikely to abuse others or to be gratuitously violent. That violence, which is the token of man's innate evil, may also be the way toward meaning is the conclusion voiced by Jack Burden:

So I went back down and stood in the garden among the black magnolia trees and the myrtles, and thought how by killing my

16. *Ibid.*, p. 188.
17. "The Achievement of Robert Warren," *South Atlantic Quarterly*, XLVII (Oct., 1948), 577.
18. *All the King's Men*, p. 464.

father I had saved my mother's soul. Then I thought how maybe I had saved my father's soul, too. Both of them had found out what they needed to know to be saved. Then I thought how all knowledge that is worth anything is maybe paid for by blood. Maybe that is the only way you can tell that a certain piece of knowledge is worth anything: it has cost some blood.[19]

Although the psychological salvation of man hinges on his coming to terms with the past, Warren, like Faulkner, is not uncritical of that past. Major Lemuel Murdock, father of the financier, had killed his opponent for the governorship evidently to silence Goodpasture's exposure of a family scandal. Now broken and senile, the Major is the miserable object of Bogan's attempt to pass off the murder as an honorable duel. By discrediting the past on the sacrosanct point of "honor," Warren employs his concept of the nature of man consistently. The corruption which the South reaps in men like Bogan Murdock comes from native bad seed, not from gratuitous circumstance or Yankee evil imported at the end of the Civil War. Faulkner's treatment of the exploitation of land and slaves as the sign of human corruption makes a similar point. In letting the father figure symbolize the past, Warren adds a significant corollary to his psychological proposition that reconciliation with the father is the means to achieve integrity. Such an acknowledgement, as Jack Burden learns, includes wholehearted acceptance of faults as well as virtues; therefore, the person so identifying himself assumes responsibility for error as well as truth, for violence as well as calm, for disorder as well as order.

Among the most ambivalent situations for Warren's characters are those in which they try to translate an idea into action, a dream into reality. The subtle equilibrium between thinking and acting, being and doing is easily distorted into violence because man's pride, fear, ignorance, and greed make it difficult to maintain a balance. Man's impulse toward order may thus by reason of his imperfect nature, plunge him into

19. *Ibid.*, p. 455.

disorder. Violence and crime, hatred and anger signify for Warren this mixed quality of human life:

> And that's the instructive fact of history,
> That evil's done for good, and in good's name—[20]

A worthy ideal alone does not insure that its realization will be worthy. Jeremiah Beaumont in *World Enough and Time* devotes himself to restoring the honor of his wife Rachel, who had been seduced by Cassius Fort. Obsessed by this single purpose, Jeremiah justifies his murder of Fort, his perjury during the trial, his betrayal of men who believed in him, and his inability to love his wife. As she dies, Rachel tells Jeremiah that he has done everything for himself: "You made me hate Fort and you used me . . . you used me to kill him, you used me, you ruined me. . . ."[21] The crime he had committed was, Jeremiah writes, "the crime of self."[22] He had erred by withdrawing from the world in order to live by the idea alone; then he had murdered to redeem the idea by action; and finally he had tried to escape his guilt by fleeing into the wilderness. When he turns homeward at last he muses that there must be a middle way, "whereby the word becomes flesh. There must be a way whereby the flesh becomes a word. Whereby loneliness becomes a communion without contamination. Whereby contamination becomes purity without exile."[23] Instead of the way of moderation he has found confusion, turmoil, and violence. From these he has learned that truth and falsehood are inextricably mixed. This knowledge he deems more efficacious than redemption, and he therefore no longer seeks to justify himself but only to suffer. It is sufficient to be aware of the conditions of human life without willing to shape them into meaning.

In *Band of Angels* the New Englander Tobias Sears endures violence and corruption as the price of trying to institute the

---

20. *Brother to Dragons*, p. 143.
21. *World Enough and Time* (New York: Random House, 1950), pp. 497-498.
22. *Ibid.*, p. 505.
23. *Ibid.*, p. 506.

ideal of freedom and justice for Negroes. Unlike Jeremiah Beaumont, Tobias is guilty of no single wilful act that precipitates disaster. Instead, he suffers the collective violence incident to the Civil War and Reconstruction. His private attempts to work out truth are thwarted by events and people over whom he has no control. Despite the impersonality of the forces which distort the idealism which he brought into the war, he does not deny his personal responsibility for its debasement. Tobias rejects Emerson's optimistic concept of a spirit of goodness which testifies to man's better nature even in his evil. He finds a more nearly accurate description of human nature in an orthodox theological position: "We went out to do fine things but there was that spirit of darkness above us. . . . We undertook to do good in the world, but we had not purged our own soul."[24] The religious view of life which has stayed alive in the South penetrates Warren's work again and again in this kind of statement. He uses the concept of man as a fallen being as an idea which is psychologically valid. It seems a measure of Warren's private rejection and of the secularization of Southern culture that the novelist only once sees the possibility of redemption in religious terms. Lettice Poindexter, Brad Tolliver's wealthy first wife in *Flood*, learns about herself through psychoanalysis. Late in the novel she re-enters to report in a letter that she has become a Roman Catholic and is content to work in a home for old people. Treated thus summarily the conversion leaves Brad untouched. The most that Warren will accept for major characters is the necessity of psychological self-knowledge as the way to understand the violence of life.

Man's effort to gain freedom for himself and others once more occupies Warren in *Wilderness*. Adam Rosenzweig, faithful to the ideal of his father who fought for freedom at Rastatt, comes to the United States to fight for the Union. Like Tobias he finds his search for truth tangled in the violence of history—riot, civil war, murder—in which he

24. *Band of Angels* (New York: Random House, 1955), p. 294.

becomes increasingly uncertain of meaning. Sure at first that "the action came out of the belief," he joins the Union army as a sutler because a crippled foot disqualifies him for military service. By removing Adam from the action Warren slows the narrative until it reads more like a recitation of a formula than a live discovery. The conclusion which finally shapes itself into words when Adam, by killing a soldier, proves to himself that he is not a coward, is consistent with Warren's sense of the absoluteness of truth in history: "He knew that he would have to try to know that the truth is unbetrayable, and that only the betrayer is ever betrayed, and then only by his own betraying."[25] The truth again is that man is carried along on a determined course of violence to the revelation that he does what he has to do not because belief precedes action but because action defines belief, the only true belief being the unity of all men in the unity of the self. In the end Adam confirms the accuracy of Aaron Blaustein's reading of history that whatever comes out of human suffering "will come only because everything is part of everything else."[26]

The significance which the violence attending the conversion of an ideal into an act has for Warren as a symptom of a serious break between intellect and feeling is made explicit by Jack Burden's contrast of Adam Stanton and Willie Stark. Adam as "the man of idea" and Willie as "the man of fact" were incomplete in their separated condition; they were therefore "doomed to destroy each other. . . ."[27] The lawlessness of Willie is actually adherence to a new order created by him on the basis of relativism elevated to an absolute principle. "The law is always too short and too tight for growing humankind," Willie explains when the Attorney General objects to protecting the auditor who misappropriated funds. "The best you can do," he continues, "is do something and then make up some law to fit and by the time that law gets

25. *Wilderness* (New York: Random House, 1961), p. 310.
26. *Ibid.*, p. 74.
27. *All the King's Men*, p. 462.

on the books you would have done something different."[28]
Like Huey Long, Willie can point to improved programs in
taxes, public health, and state highways as the ends to justify
his means. He has practiced disorder for the sake of order. In
assuming that the world is merely raw material for his action
to shape, Willie denies that there is any continuity of order
and ideas from the past into the future. He rejects accumulated human tradition and confuses violence with creativity.

To Adam Stanton, however, this ambivalence is immoral.
Trained in medicine, he wants human beings to behave with
the predictability of atoms. His belief in inflexible standards
makes it inevitable that he and Willie will clash violently
when they meet on the same issue. Like Jeremiah Beaumont,
Adam cannot maintain the purity of his position without
action when his honor has been put in doubt, as it has by
Willie's taking Anne for his mistress and offering Adam the
directorship of a new memorial hospital. He fatally wounds
Willie and is in turn shot down. The attempt to separate the
act from the ideal or the ideal from the act ends in violence
because one without the other is a violation of the unity of
life. But Warren sees man always beset by the terror of not
knowing how to combine the ideal and the actual construc-
tively.

The devastating power of the unprincipled intellect when
linked with modern means of communication is portrayed in
The Cave. Isaac Sumpter epitomizes the educated, highly in-
telligent, secular man who knows everything except how to
live. His ability to manipulate others through their basest
motives of greed and sensation-seeking produces an orgy of
cheap, crude violence. Human tragedy becomes a commodity
for sale, and the radio and newspapers which peddle it are the
ultimate violation of decent privacy. The days and nights
which Isaac spends in the cave where Jasper Harrick has been
trapped, relaying to the spectators his false version of the

28. *Ibid.*, p. 145.

reality within the cave, form a parable of the fascistic mind as powerful as *All the King's Men*. Because he is afraid to crawl through a dangerous passage in the cave to reach Jasper, Isaac rationalizes that Jasper is already dead and merely pretends to communicate with him. Late in the rescue work, McCarland Sumpter, Isaac's father, crawls back to Jasper and finds him dead but still warm. The enormity of his son's deception is clear, and the ancient sacrifice offered by Abraham becomes for McCarland the sacrifice of his integrity. He corroborates Isaac's lies. Thus in his love McCarland corrupts the ideal of moral duty which might have appealed to his son, who earlier had scoffed at the possibility of a modern enactment of Abraham's obedience.

The ruthlessness of Bogan Murdock, the negativism of Percy Munn, and the single-mindedness of Jeremiah Beaumont characterize Isaac. He treats those around him as abstractions because he has no knowledge of himself as a person; in fact, his idea of himself is so untrue that it obscures and distorts even the shadows of reality which flicker across the walls of the cave. In Isaac the fatal coldness that afflicted Mr. Munn is combined with a rejection of the father who, in this instance, signifies the faith of the past. McCarland, a preacher, has never been able to communicate his faith to his son and, as the novel develops, Warren shows that even the man of faith carries violence in his heart. This violence comes to a focus in Jasper, the son of Old Jack Harrick. As McCarland's rival, Old Jack had seduced the woman McCarland married. The two men have lived as friends, but the crisis precipitated by Jasper's accident discloses the consequences of emotions which they have concealed through the years. When Jasper's death is confirmed, both confess that in spirit they have been murderers desiring this outcome: McCarland because Jasper was the son of his rival; Harrick because the death of Jasper, of whom he had always been jealous, seemed a substitute for his own death. In facing their guilt both men find that their conflicts have been resolved. McCarland has renewed his faith, and Harrick is unafraid to die. Warren does not make the reconciliation of these men to one another and to themselves a wholesale endorsement of the past as a reservoir of religious faith, but he clearly allows them a portion of order and peace which is denied to Isaac, who remains outside the tradition. Warren thus brings the two fathers to the knowledge which he repeatedly lets violence reveal: man's perception of truth is so partial that he can never presume to act in purity, and the fear of non-being leads him to betray others for his own security.

Although Warren holds the individual responsible for the violence with which he destroys himself and others, he also recognizes the pressure by which masses of men determine the action of individuals. Groups generate a force of their own which the individual cannot control. Percy Munn feels this energy of the crowd in the trainload of people coming to the political rally at Bardsville, and he resents the pressure "that was human because it was made by human beings, but was inhuman, too, because you could not isolate and blame any one of those human beings who made it."[29] As an old man Jack Harrick hates the image of himself as a "heller" famous for lusty loves, an image which both he and his community had created. He had needed this portrait to convince himself that his vigor was such that he would never die and pass into the nothingness which he secretly knew lay at the center of himself; the people of the community had needed it to substitute for the strength and freedom they lacked in themselves.

The exploitation practiced by men like Willie Stark and Isaac Sumpter is supported by the desires of men weaker than they but no less violent. People will believe Isaac because, as Jack Harrick explains, "Folks believe what they want to believe."[30] And Isaac knows the level of vicariously experienced danger, fear, despair, and death which will most stimulate and entertain them. The political empire of Willie rises on the thwarted will to power of every voter he harangues.

29. *Night Rider*, pp. 2-3.
30. *The Cave* (New York: Random House, 1950), p. 384.

In the long run they have no more scruples about how power is exercised than he. The ambiguous relationship between the violence of the individual and of the mass reveals the complex connections between the person and the formal organization of his life in political and social groups. Warren's reading of the past and of the nature of man is a warning against the assumption that human life can ever be easily freed from violence and distortion.

In addition to treating the problem of violence through specific examples of social and economic injustice in Southern history, Warren recognizes the increasing mechanization and urbanization of the South as a general source of turbulence. Jeff York in "The Patented Gate and the Mean Hamburger" commits suicide at his farm to avoid the cramped town life to which his wife aspires.[31] The Seven Dwarfs Motel with its fake fantasy and ugly advertising betokens for Brad Tolliver a new commercial crudeness in the South. In *All the King's Men*, Jack Burden remarks that "this is the country where the age of the internal combustion engine has come into its own. . . . Where the eight-cylinder jobs come roaring round the curves in the red hills and scatter the gravel like spray. . . ."[32] Nature itself is mechanical in the images which describe the glade outside the cave where Jasper Harrick is trapped. The locusts make a "grinding metallic sound" like a buzz saw. Their "remorseless whir" fills the valley with racking noise like the whine of a factory.[33]

Warren regrets the changes brought by industry, but he does not imagine that farms are utopian. Only twice—in the stories of Willie Proudfit in *Night Rider* and of Ashby Wyndham in *At Heaven's Gate*—does Warren picture rural people as possessing preternatural wisdom and calm. And in both instances these qualities have been gained only by a passage through violence. Willie Proudfit, the farmer with whom

31. "The Patented Gate and the Mean Hamburger," *The Circus in the Attic and Other Stories* (New York, Harcourt, Brace and Company, 1947), pp. 120-133.
32. *All the King's Men*, p. 4.
33. *The Cave*, p. 4.

Percy Munn hides when he is suspected of killing a key witness in a case against the Protective Association, had come
back to the land only after rejecting his parents and wandering through the West. In the delirium of a fever he had pictured a green country where he refreshed himself, a land he
actually found in Kentucky. "I come over the hill, down the
road," Willie tells Mr. Munn, "and thar was the grass and the
trees standen green. Lak hit is, and lak hit come to me that
time."[34] Proudfit enjoys the kind of harmony between man
and place which Faulkner also celebrates, but his mystical
relation to the land is a rarefied agrarianism which the disturbed tobacco farmers do not share. Proudfit's nephew feels
that the union has been broken and that "the way folks been
revelen and carren on" has put a curse on the land for which
the threatening drought is punishment. Although Warren
presents the agrarian way idyllically in the Proudfit household, there is nothing to suggest that the program can be en-
acted by social reform, certainly not by group action which
violates the rights of individuals. Instead, Munn's belief that
the idea which bound the men together in the Association
"would get justice for all of them"—even eventually for men
whose tobacco beds were scraped—explodes into violence.

Ashby Wyndham's autobiography is a record in miniature
of the pattern of the repudiation of parents, the flight from
home, and the return with love which Warren in later novels
assigns to central characters. Like the Proudfits, Ashby inter-
prets the violence of his behavior as a judgment of God on his
wrath and wickedness. After he is jailed for his part in a
skirmish in which a policeman is shot, Ashby refuses to be
released through the influence of a cousin who is one of
Bogan Murdock's henchmen. "Man's rightness ain't nuthin to
me," Ashby declares. "It is trash and a deceivin. I am here of
a God rightness, and here I lay."[35] In these simple characters
the step from violence to psychological rebirth is direct. In
subsequent novels Warren develops many-dimensioned char-

34. *Night Rider*, p. 426.
35. *At Heaven's Gate*, p. 334.

acters whose response to violence is correspondingly complex.

With men like Willie Proudfit and Jeremiah Beaumont who run away to the wilderness to escape violence, Warren supports the myth of the innocence of the land, but he also uses the grotesque to discredit this idea. In *World Enough and Time* Jeremiah and Rachel flee to the hide-out of the river pirate La Grand' Bosse or Ole Big Hump, a monster generated by the swamps and jungles of Louisiana or by the mixed bloods of New Orleans. He looks like a "great brute of the depth that swagged up from the blind, primal mud to reach the light and wallow in the stagnant flood, festooned with algae and the bright slime, with his scaled, armored, horny back just awash, like a log."[36] His hideous appearance, his strength, his ruthlessness, his treachery, and his gargantuan self-indulgence have become legends. But the coming of the steamboat ended his plundering. On the river and on the land the machine made other kinds of robbery profitable. In contrast to Willie Proudfit or Ashby Wyndham, Ole Big Hump is a beast in the Garden, a grotesque monster whose presence adulterates the dream of beauty and truth in the land. Frog-Eye in *Flood* is a similar primordial swamp creature. He, however, is capable of a moment of sensitivity when he refuses to attack Lettice whom he sees weeping as she lies by her drunk husband.

Warren is most a part of the Southern tradition when he makes a reconciliation with the past the way to integrity in the present. This acceptance includes a feeling of guilt and responsibility for the faults of the past. These flaws are not specifically localized in slavery and the exploitation of the land as they are in Faulkner. There is simply a general recognition that, given man's defective nature, one generation only with difficulty conveys its ideals to another. Warren therefore chooses incidents from Southern history not for their historical but for their psychological implications. This use of history assures him a kind of universality, but it falls short of the com-

36. *World Enough and Time*, p. 471.

prehensive view achieved by Faulkner in deeply meditating on the Southern past until its inextricable relations to the present appear as commentary on the totality of human life. The fact that the situation in *All the King's Men* touches the problem of force and freedom which appears throughout the American experience accounts for much of the power of this novel. In the same respect, *Band of Angels* is less successful because the historical problem of slavery chiefly furnishes melodramatic details rather than an illumination of present maladjustments as rooted in the past. Again, in *Flood* Fiddlersburg is not a convincing epitome of the South because the lives of the townspeople remain static in the thoughts of Brad Tolliver. When Brad tries to find out what Fiddlersburg means to him, he is defeated by his inability to recognize the destruction inherent in his hatred of a brutal father who came from the swamp country to usurp power and position in Fiddlersburg. All he can do finally is to admit that he is rooted in the town and that he had found a substitute father in the tailor Israel Goldfarb; he cannot convert these attachments into art whether in fiction or in a film script. When past and present are utterly separated as represented by the rejection of the father, violence inevitably occurs.

The historical germ also carries with it certain forms of ready-made violence which Warren skilfully exploits. In *World Enough and Time*, for example, he reconstructs the frontier with quarrels and brawls, the law of hard fists, and the language of boasts and roars. Warren uses this material primarily for its action rather than for the boisterous amusement which the Southwest humorists found in it. The conventions of violence on the frontier easily support the characterization of such men as Carlos Bumps and Lancaster Sugg. In the novels set during the Civil War, however, Warren makes little use of mass violence on the battlefield. He chooses to work out the theme of self-discovery in the private violence of individuals.

In Warren's fiction as a whole violence originates in an

excess of thought or feeling coupled with insufficient self-knowledge. Its meaning, however, derives from the meditation of the participants or the spectators. More violence appears on-stage in Warren's work than in Faulkner's, but both authors elaborate their comments on this action either directly or indirectly through narrative devices. Warren, for example, invents activities for the chief characters which force them to make formal statements of meaning. Jack Burden writes the autobiography of Cass Mastern, and Jeremiah Beaumont prepares a journal. These documents emphasize the passage of violence from the past to the present with the burden of knowledge which the present has to recover.

Geographically, Warren sets most of his fiction in the border states of Kentucky and Tennessee where he has lived. Although he now lives in New England, he has never written a novel which is not rooted in the people, the land, and the history of the South. His ear for speech and eye for behavior particularizes especially the back-country people of the Kentucky-Tennessee hills or Louisiana farms, people never far from violence in settling differences and rectifying injuries. The tobacco farmer Trevelyan remonstrates, "Since I got too big for my pappy to beat, ain't no man ever named to me whut I could do and whut I couldn't do."[37] Uncle Lew believes that his club foot was good enough "to tromp and scrouge on Lem Burdock's shoulders by God, till the neck bones scrunched."[38] Accurate delineation of the local scene, however, does not make Warren's work autobiographical or sociological. Its expression of a particular place and people is the ground of the meaning which emerges from the action of the imagination on the immediate. The presence of the local and the immediate, in fact, distinguishes the fiction of each of the contemporary Southern writers to be considered in this study. However far they may range in distortion, fantasy, or grotesquerie, they are not dealing with picture-painted backgrounds.

37. *Night Rider*, p. 78.
38. *At Heaven's Gate*, p. 87.

In all times and places, man as Warren sees him is separated from his genuine self, and this inner disharmony creates the violence of events and personal relationships. Each instance of violence illustrates man's real condition of being divided within himself and consequently from others. In his odyssey he must revisit the past in the symbol of the father and carry it with him. Thus joined with history, his narrow constricted ego can be enlarged into a responsible self in the human community. Only then will systems of polity really contain order.

In quasi-theological terms, Warren might be said to find the fall from innocence fortunate because it brings man to the knowledge of his identity which redeems him from alienation and disunity. If man elects to live by action or by idea alone, a disjunction which charactizes contemporary life, he is doomed to destroy himself and those around him. Only a knowledge of self which incorporates an acceptance of the past can protect him from the danger of extremes. Warren's particular contribution to Southern fiction is the development of a pattern which not only reveals the psychological origin of the violence that disfigures human life but also provides for its control and reorientation.

II. The test by fire: Flannery O'Connor

Among the young Southern writers whose fiction began to appear in the late forties, Flannery O'Connor is notable for the precision with which she defines the intention of her work and the power with which she dramatizes her ideas. Sin, guilt, mercy, and redemption are the realities of human life for her, and the lives of her characters are violent, mean, frustrated, twisted, and fragmented because man is a sinner. He cannot escape the consequences of his pride and anger, sloth and greed except by the ministration of divine love and mercy. As Caroline Gordon notes, Miss O'Connor is unique among recent writers for the definite and clear support which she draws from orthodox theology. For Miss O'Connor there is no explanation for the behavior of man except in terms of his relation to God. The sociology of poverty and the psychology of fear may help to interpret the action, but they never obscure the central drama—man's flight and God's pursuit. The love which corrects man's perversion often appears as a holy wrath. Its visitation cannot be explained by the social sciences or by literary art. Deep in Miss O'Connor's fiction lies the wonder that man matters sufficiently for God to care. This wonder never emerges as propaganda; it comes forth as literature with the power to move the reader to believe in The Misfit, the Greenleafs, Haze Motes, and Francis Marion Tarwater.

In an essay contributed to a symposium on the contemporary American novel, Miss O'Connor discusses her reasons for writing about people who are materially and spiritually afflicted. She underscores the relation between culture and belief in the twentieth century which compels this choice. Her statement might well be the credo of all writers, the unbelieving as well as the believing, who have employed violence and grotesqueness in contemporary literature for serious purposes:

The novelist with Christian concerns will find in modern life distortions which are repugnant to him, and his problem will be to make these appear as distortions to an audience which is used to seeing them as natural; and he may well be forced to take over more violent means to get his vision across to this hostile audience. When you can assume that your audience holds the same beliefs you do, you can relax a little and use more normal ways of talking to it; when you have to assume that it does not, then you have to make your vision apparent by shock—to the hard

1. "With a Glitter of Evil" (review of *A Good Man Is Hard to Find*), *New York Times Book Review*, June 12, 1955, p. 5, and "Flannery O'Connor's *Wise Blood*," *Critique*, II (Fall, 1958), 9.

of hearing you shout, and for the almost blind you draw large and startling figures.[2]

Implicit in this method of enlargement is the danger of creating caricatures who evoke no response from the reader instead of characters who provoke pity and compassion or even disgust. Erskine Caldwell, it has been noted, errs on the side of dehumanizing his people when their lusts and afflictions are exaggerated. In the estimate of some readers and critics, Miss O'Connor commits the same error by exaggerating spiritual anomalies. Her approach, it must be acknowledged however, contains two corrective elements: her firmly objective treatment of the characters and the dominant theme of man in relation to an absolute which transcends the immediate confusion and ruin.

In her essay Miss O'Connor further makes clear that the grotesque in her work is not a peculiar Southern preoccupation, but that, like violence, it serves to expose the condition of man which she believes an increasingly secular culture ignores. "My own feeling is," she remarks, "that writers who see by the light of their Christian faith will have, in these times, the sharpest eyes for the grotesque, for the perverse, and for the unacceptable."[3] They will be most sensitive to these distortions because they look unflinchingly at what is real. And for these writers, reality begins in a sense that life is mysterious, that what we do not understand is more important than what we know. They have a prophetic vision which "is a matter of seeing far things close up. The prophet is a realist of distances, and it is this kind of realism that you find in the best modern instances of the grotesque."[4] Having seen the end which awaits the weariness and futility of the present, these writers must report in terms which will attract attention. At this point the requirements of religion and of art may clash,

2. "The Fiction Writer and His Country," *The Living Novel: A Symposium*, ed. Granville Hicks (New York: Macmillan, 1957), pp. 162-163.
3. *Ibid.*, p. 162.
4. Flannery O'Connor, "Some Aspects of the Grotesque in Southern Fiction," address at Macon, Georgia, October 27, 1960.

and instruction may defeat imagination. But in Miss O'Connor's fiction dramatic conflicts involve moral judgment, and morality envisioned in dramatic conflicts becomes newly compelling.

In making violence a religious evaluation of modern life, Miss O'Connor is more akin to Robert Penn Warren than to any other writer among the young Southerners. The effect of moral neutrality created by some who deal with limited aesthetic and psychological problems is not characteristic of her work. This is not to say that she is a religious propagandist but rather that she makes more clear than do they the moral basis from which she proceeds. This foundation is her guarantee of freedom to examine every aspect of life with an artist's wholeness and truthfulness. The integrity of the writer, she insists, depends upon his honest attention to literal facts at the natural level, for these are the only building materials which he has, and he cannot construct without knowing exactly their dimensions. In a brief review of Teilhard de Chardin's *The Phenomenon of Man*, Miss O'Connor reiterates this principle of creative insight; prophetic vision, whether achieved by the poet or the scientist, is the result of an attempt to "penetrate matter until spirit is revealed in it."[5]

Miss O'Connor writes with a strong sense of place. Her country is Georgia, where she was born in Savannah in 1925. Following her graduation from Georgia State College for Women, she spent two years studying creative writing with Paul Engle at the State University of Iowa. After a brief stay in New York she returned to Milledgeville, Georgia, where she lives with her mother on a farm.[*] She twice received a *Kenyon Review* Fellowship in Creative Writing, and in 1959 she held a Ford Foundation Fellowship for creative writers.

5. See "The Church and the Fiction Writer," *America*, XC (March 30, 1957), 733, and review of *The Phenomenon of Man*, *American Scholar*, XXX (Fall, 1961), 618.

[*] Just as this book went to press, word was received of the death of Miss O'Connor. Through several years of poor health Miss O'Connor had continued writing, never asking relief from the demands of the integrity of her art. Her early death thus unfortunately deprives us of the additional works of high quality which she would have completed.

Her home obviously supplied the primary materials for her
fiction: the exigencies of life on the farm, especially when
viewed through the commonsensical wit of her mother; the
eccentricities of rural people, white and Negro, who work
there as "hired hands"; and the banalities of small-town life.
Her characters think and talk in the idiom and drawl of the
back country; they speak from folk knowledge about everything from remedies for ailments to Old Testament proph-
ecies.

In her two novels, *Wise Blood* (1952) and *The Violent
Bear It Away* (1960), Miss O'Connor explores the madness of
those who are possessed by religion. The short stories collected in *A Good Man Is Hard to Find* (1955) scrutinize the
afflicted spirits of criminals, hypocrites, abandoned children,
and harassed parents in conditions made worse by ugliness,
poverty, and ignorance. One of the realities of Southern life
of which Miss O'Connor is most certain is that sentiment will
not save it. In her work, cities are evil, but the simplicities of
romantic agrarianism border on idiocy; the historical past is
Sally Poker Sash's grandfather to whom "the past and the
future were the same thing . . ., one forgotten and the other
not remembered," and family loyalty has become deception
and bickering.[6] A veneer of pretense covers most human relationships and masks people from their true selves. To peel
back this veneer and reveal the twisted and demonic human
nature below is the special function of violence in Miss O'Connor's fiction.

Painful as this revelation is, it is not without humor, for the
matter-of-fact tone in which characters and narrator speak
is a buffer between the violence of the action and the horror
which might be the reader's natural reaction. The flat tone reflects a finely balanced objectivity which is never blurred by
the woes of the characters. They ask for sympathy and receive
justice. Because Miss O'Connor abhors sentimentality, the

6. "A Late Encounter with the Enemy," *A Good Man Is Hard to Find*
(New York: Harcourt, Brace and Company, 1955), p. 161.

omniscient point of view which she frequently adopts has an edge of sour amusement at the predicament of man. She always sees the preposterous and the perverse for what they are. They cannot be turned into order by mere reversal but must undergo transformation. The struggle is comic both at short range and at long. Close up the characters are stubbornly foolish and absurd; ultimately—against their wills—they reveal the workings of eternal redemption. The kind of people whom Caldwell leaves floundering as grotesques in a world they never made become for Miss O'Connor instruments of the Divine Will. Thus the irony which she practices is that of paradox rather than simple contradiction.

One of the most disturbing aspects of violence in Miss O'Connor's fiction is its seeming gratuitousness. If violence is unmotivated, then man must be inescapably irrational and brutal, incapable of restraint. This kind of explanation would be in some respects a more comfortable view of man than the one Miss O'Connor illustrates with The Misfit in "A Good Man Is Hard to Find." The Misfit is an escaped criminal who cannot even remember having murdered his father. By the end of the story he and his henchmen have killed a family of six as matter-of-factly as if they were having target practice. In the crisis the grandmother, a kind of universal mother and elderly busybody, proves abjectly inadequate to match her sudden compassion for The Misfit with his despair. Despite his pathological mind, The Misfit has gone to the core of the problem of redemption, where, Miss O'Connor states, "for me the meaning of life is centered. . . ."[7] He has seen the alternatives posed by Christ's raising the dead:

If He did what He said, then it's nothing for you to do but thow away everything and follow Him, and if He didn't, then it's nothing for you to do but enjoy the few minutes you got left the best way you can—by killing somebody or burning down his house or doing some other meanness to him. No pleasure but meanness. . . . [8]

7. "The Fiction Writer and His Country," p. 161.
8. "A Good Man Is Hard to Find," *A Good Man Is Hard to Find*, p. 28.

This is the conclusion toward which Robert Penn Warren leads his characters, but he always stops them short by substituting knowledge for redemption. The violence of his characters never expresses the stark clarity of the orthodox answer with which Miss O'Connor's characters struggle.

The horrifying revelation which Miss O'Connor springs in this story is that the violence which seemed aimless is really the logical result of The Misfit's decision, a choice which differs from the common one of mankind only in the lucidity with which it has been made and the steadiness with which it has been followed. The Misfit is an enlarged drawing of the despair, the murderous impulses, and the greed for pleasure which characterize the unbelieving man. He also sits in judgment on his choice. When one of his accomplices shows enthusiasm for shooting people, The Misfit reprimands him: "Shut up, Bobby Lee. It's no real pleasure in life."[9] The relation between the theme of lost man and violence worked out in this story dominates Miss O'Connor's fiction.

Ignorant, immature, or childishly simple characters are gripped by and in turn grapple with problems of immense theological complexity. By using untutored characters Miss O'Connor points out that these problems are both vastly complicated and paradoxically simple. These people can state in the folk idiom all that is problematic about human life. "Jesus," The Misfit declares, "thown everything off balance."[10] History has been invaded by a dimension beyond the human, and man is thus defenseless. Uncertain about life and anxious about death, he must make a radical choice between believing and not believing. Violence emphasizes the urgency of this choice. Even if he refuses to choose, violence exacerbates his conscience to remind him that he cannot escape the conditions of the spiritual order which he occupies.

In Miss O'Connor's short stories the secular expression of man's separation from God often takes the form of corrosive

9. *Ibid.*, p. 29.
10. *Ibid.*, p. 27.

tension between parents and children, from which violence as an act or an attitude results. In the conflict between generations the complacency and conservatism of the old is pitted against the dissatisfaction and experimentalism of the new; the elders accept the answers they were given, but the young people deny these answers and persist in asking questions. The parents who have no real wisdom merely incite rebellion and disgust by mouthing platitudes. Their narrow-mindedness is a perpetual irritant to their sons and daughters. For the most part the violence between generations is restricted to words or gestures, which serve also as devices of characterization, as foreshadowing, and as criticism of sentimental traditions about the home and history. Joy Hopewell in "Good Country People" is representative of the young adults who hate their mothers but yet are dependent upon them. Fortified by a doctorate in philosophy, Joy rages at the truisms by which her mother solves problems: "Nothing is perfect." "That is life!" "Other people have their opinions too." The fact that Mrs. Hopewell and the other mothers are impervious to the hatred concentrates the venom. The parents have never been alive, and the children poison themselves with their own frustration. Mrs. May's sons in "Greenleaf" snarl like caged, mistreated animals. On a small scale this family suggests the Gants who also had been over-advised and under-loved by a woman who in dedicating herself to the practical thought she was devoting herself to the real. "I wouldn't milk a cow to save your soul from hell," Wesley May murmurs to his mother.[11]

The brattishness of Mrs. Cope's child and the three trespassing boys in "A Circle in the Fire" deepens into malevolence. Their evil spirits circle around Mrs. Cope until she is almost reduced to gibbering fear. Her boasts that she can cope with whatever fate sends go up with the flames of the fire which the boys set in her woods. She is powerless before the blank eyes of boys who can imagine a parking lot where

11. "Greenleaf," *Kenyon Review*, XVIII (Summer, 1956), 395.

her precious trees now stand. Mere possessiveness like Mrs. Cope's, however, will not protect the country from the invading cities.

All sentiment about duty and respect between generations is blasted by the violent expression of hatred. In "The Life You Save May Be Your Own" the boy hitchhiker who rides with Mr. Shiftlet appears only briefly, but he sharply challenges Mr. Shiftlet's saccharine lecture on the duty a son owes to his mother. Mr. Shiftlet asserts that his own mother was "an angel of Gawd." The boy counters angrily, "You go to the devil! My old woman is a flea bag and yours is a stinking pole cat!"[12] The hostility between another pair, young Mary Fortune Pitts and her grandfather in "A View of the Woods," is extreme. Grandfather as the past cannot alienate the girl from her family—and the present. In their conflict the old man and the granddaughter finally kill one another, thus enacting a violent parable of the viciousness of a pride in the past which is nothing more than self-seeking, greed, and envy.

The past is alien to Miss O'Connor's young people. Because it threatens their being alive in the present, they seek no relationship with it through their elders. The accommodation of parent and child which Robert Penn Warren sees as a measure of health never occurs in Miss O'Connor's work, where friction is ever-present. This hostility has a specific social focus in "Everything That Rises Must Converge." Julian, another of Miss O'Connor's young people just getting started as a writer, hates his mother's push-button responses, phrased as clichés. "Rome wasn't built in a day" defends her son's lack of success, and "I tell you, the bottom rail is on the top" explains world events. About Negroes she is sure: "They should rise, yes, but on their own side of the fence."[13] Julian feels appointed by his intelligence, sensitivity, and education to rescue his mother from prejudice and to preserve the real quality of his aristocratic past (a great-grandfather had been governor of the

12. *A Good Man Is Hard to Find*, p. 67.
13. "Everything That Rises Must Converge," *New World Writing* 19 (New York: J. B. Lippincott Company, 1961), 75, 76, 77.

state). He relishes the embarrassment of his mother at the sight of a Negro woman wearing a hat like hers, but she refuses the lesson of alikeness and condescends from her superiority to play games with the Negro's little boy. Despite Julian's warnings she must continue the role of white mistress of the plantation by giving the boy a penny. For this insult she is struck by the Negro mother and dies within the hour. The impasse compounded by Julian's loveless ideal and his mother's complacency destroys both the present and the past as the whites visualize them. Only the rebellious Negro wins, for she has stalked off unaware of the consequences of her action.

The terms of life whether for children or for adults rarely include peace or reconciliation. Instead, existence is a series of malevolent frustrations which prove that man is alienated not only from God and human kind but also from nature. The women in particular feel embattled. The farms which they manage—the workers, the land and the crops, the stock, the financing—appear wilfully recalcitrant. Violence is imminent in the grimness. Mrs. Cope pulls weeds "as if they were an evil sent directly by the devil to destroy the place."[14] The trees on the horizons enclose the land like a fortress described at various times as black or granite.[15] Although Mrs. May can take satisfaction in the order she has imposed on her farm, she knows that "the weather is against you and the dirt is against you and the help is against you. . . . There's nothing for it but an iron hand!"[16]

From the familiar features of nature Miss O'Connor creates numerous metaphors and similes which suggest violence. Objects or events in nature, such as storms, may in themselves be violent, but she is concerned with them as tokens of the tensions within man. The images may describe emotions or locales, or they may be quick character sketches that catch both the salient quality of the person and the author's attitude toward him, providing at one stroke the picture and the tone.

14. "A Circle in the Fire," *A Good Man Is Hard to Find*, p. 131.
15. *Ibid.*, pp. 151, 154.
16. "Greenleaf," p. 396.

In one sentence, for example, she projects the fierceness and intractability of Mason Tarwater, the back-country prophet in *The Violent Bear It Away*: "He was a bull-like old man with a short head set directly into his shoulders and silver protruding eyes that looked like two fish straining to get out of a net of red threads."[17] When Mrs. Crater in "The Life You Save May Be Your Own" agrees to buy paint for the old car, the smile of the well-named Mr. Shiftlet stretches "like a weary snake waking up by a fire."[18] The snake again connotes the malign when the train which has taken Nelson and his grandfather of "The Artificial Nigger" into the wickedness of Atlanta disappears like a serpent gliding into the woods.[19]

To suggest the fury which threatens to explode out of the emotions and actions of her characters Miss O'Connor often bases images on the sun. In simple description this body may menace the scene like the scorching balls of light in Van Gogh's paintings. *The Violent Bear It Away*, for example, opens with the sun "furious white" and closes with it "red and mammoth."[20] In comparisons the color and heat and glare of the sun evoke the complex connections between the physical and the metaphysical in human life. During a weekend visit from her cousins, the child in "A Temple of the Holy Ghost" is agitated by the inexplicable mixture of beauty and ugliness in life which she apprehends while the others gabble on. She must deal with the moving idea that she is a Temple of the Holy Ghost and with the disturbing fact of the carnival hermaphrodite. In her perplexity the girl sees the setting sun as "a huge red ball like an elevated Host drenched in blood."[21] Just before the angry boys in "A Circle in the Fire" fulfil Mrs. Cope's deepest dread by setting fire to the woods, the sun appears a foreboding white, "a white hole like an opening for the wind to escape through in a sky a little darker than itself,

17. *The Violent Bear It Away* (New York: Farrar, Straus and Cudahy, 1960), p. 10.
18. *A Good Man Is Hard to Find*, p. 63.
19. *Ibid.*, p. 129.
20. *The Violent Bear It Away*, pp. 44, 235.
21. *A Good Man Is Hard to Find*, p. 101.

and the tops of the trees were black against the glare."[22] The sun as a purifying and destructive agent had been turned on Mason Tarwater when he set out to prophesy from his fury that "the world would see the sun burst in blood and fire." Instead the frenzied man had seen a finger of fire thrust out and had felt his blood burn dry.[23] These sun-images point a parallel between the life-giving and life-taking physical energy of the sun and the creative and destructive spiritual energy which inflames many of the characters. Miss O'Connor uses nature imagery unobtrusively but exactly to support her vision of the rage of man.

Because the violence which occurs in Miss O'Connor's work derives almost exclusively from relations with the supernatural, it is rare that nature is the sole source of violent power. In "Greenleaf," however, the scrub bull loose on Mrs. May's farm is the ancient symbol of sex. Silvered by the moonlight and tossing a hedge wreath on his horns, he stands outside Mrs. May's bedroom window "like some patient god come down to woo her."[24] Behind him stand his owners, the Greenleaf sons—and the host of those with animal energy who will devour the effete and unproductive like Mrs. May's sons. Dreams of dispossession and death presage the destruction. Death comes in a lurid rite of spring in which the bull "like a wild tormented lover" impales Mrs. May, one of his horns curling around her side and holding her in a fatal embrace. The violence welds together the hatred of the sons for the mother and the vulgar pride of the mother. The cumulative selfishness is fully exposed in the strange courtship, the sudden disaster, and the stark physical details. Such an emphatic treatment of the sensations of violence is uncharacteristic of Miss O'Connor's fiction, for the act is generally subordinate to the disturbed state of the person committing it.

The struggle with nature may involve complicated moral demands which subject the characters to violence. When

22. *Ibid.*, p. 151.
23. *The Violent Bear It Away*, pp. 5-6.
24. "Greenleaf," p. 384.

Father Flynn in "The Displaced Person" arranges for the Guizacs, a family of displaced Poles, to work for Mrs. Mc-Intyre, he upsets the decorum of the entire farm: the tenant Shortleys fear the foreigners as barbaric agents of Satan; the Negroes are unsettled by the possibility of importing a white Polish wife; Mrs. McIntyre is disturbed by the priest's insistence that her obligation to the refugees is also an obligation to the Lord. Mrs. Shortley's primitivistic solution is a vision which instructs her to prophesy the destruction of the wicked, the foreign, but she dies twisted by a paralytic stroke. Mrs. McIntyre also is destroyed by her refusal to be concerned about the refugees. Failing to warn Mr. Guizac when a tractor rolls toward him, she feels responsible for his death and disintegrates under her burden of guilt. By violence and death Miss O'Connor emphasizes her view that the universe is inexorably moral. Whether this fact is denied out of ignorance and superstition or out of expediency it remains an active and inviolable principle. Denial of it is tantamount to death, as Mrs. Shortley, Mrs. McIntyre, and The Misfit learn.

The violence or the grotesque behavior most disruptive to human relations is that which betrays others through deception. In a pair of stories, "The Life You Save May Be Your Own" and "Good Country People," Miss O'Connor ironically reverses the usual role of the hypocrite. The carefully laid campaign of pious-speaking Tom Shiftlet nets him Mrs. Crater's old car, her deaf daughter, and $17.50. His moral intelligence, which he considers the distinguishing trait of man, is not disturbed when he abandons Lucynell at their first stop. More complicated is the double deception of Joy Hopewell by the Bible salesman. Convinced that her atheism and intelligence make her superior to country people, she arranges a tryst with the salesman, intending to seduce him to the shame of his religious scruples. The folk humor of the theme of the man-who-comes-apart develops grotesque overtones when the young man packs Joy's artificial leg in his suitcase along with the hollow Bible which contains a flask of whiskey

and a deck of cards, and departs, remarking that he had once
got a woman's glass eye in this way. This salesman who had
announced himself at the door as wanting to devote his life
to "Chrustion service" destroys the young woman's intellectual
pride. He taunts her that the lack of belief to which she has
come by laborious study was his from the beginning. These
betrayals are so amusing in tone that it is almost possible to
forget that they deal with the lost, the damned, the proud,
and the angry.

In "The Artificial Nigger" the grandfather's refusal to recognize his grandson when the boy accidentally knocks down
a shopper destroys the boy's trust and turns his love into hate.
Mr. Head shudders at the black future which faces him. His
alienation from Nelson is an analogy for the abandoned condition of man and provides the occasion for an act of mercy.
When the two are reconciled, the grandfather has a sense of
having been saved from the violence of a depravity which he
had never before recognized in himself. The betrayal which
leads the child Harry Ashfield in "The River" to drown himself represents a lifetime of neglect by his parents. The dreariness of his life in an unkempt apartment with his parents'
hangovers, their indifference, and the succession of women
paid to look after him makes him susceptible to the young
preacher who promises that baptism will make him count and
that the river will lead to the Kingdom of Christ. For the child
the Kingdom is the only home which has ever been offered
him. In thus giving children over to misery and violence, the
adults enact the insensitivity and cruelty of unredeemed
human nature, a portrayal compounded by the scrubbiness
and nastiness of the children.

The most violent and unattractive characters in Miss
O'Connor's work are those obsessed by religious fervor. They
are infected with Bible Belt literalism in its most virulent, un-
controlled, and hysterical form. In its grip they are capable
of exploitation and violation of others, of fraud and self-mutilation, or arson and murder. But Miss O'Connor does not stop

with the simple equation that man corrupts even his religion;
indeed his very corruption may be a sign of his thirst for right-
eousness. The brutality and savagery of these people are
shocking statements to recall the reader's attention to the un-
compromising primacy of God's demands. Their repelling behavior cuts through all conventional concepts and attitudes
to make clear the fundamental point that religion profoundly
reorders human life. Pleasantness and prettiness, respectability and proper manners have nothing to do with the reality
of man's need for redemption. Nor can the reader take literary
comfort in assuming that Miss O'Connor is engaged in a satiric
demonstration of primitive emotionalism among backwoods
Georgians. In some of the short stories, it is true, she exploits
the satiric potential of frenetic religiosity. Mrs. Greenleaf's
prayer healing, for example, is made ridiculous as the fat
woman sprawls on the ground bellowing over newspaper
clippings of violent crimes and accidents which she has
buried. At the same time her employer Mrs. May is jabbed by
the author as "a good Christian woman with a large respect
for religion, though she did not, of course, believe any of it
was true."[25]

In the novels *Wise Blood* and *The Violent Bear It Away*,
violence and grotesqueness are the means for accomplishing
in fiction a vision not unlike Kierkegaard's, one which con-
fronts man with the uncomfortable demands of genuine Christian faith. Miss O'Connor intends to dramatize the discovery
which, in the words of Denis de Rougemont, stunned the
Danish theologian: "We have distorted Christianity, we have
held it cheap, instead of recognizing that we are unworthy of
it and admitting that we refuse to pay its price."[26] In gruesome incidents and hysterical characters she finds realities
which secular culture prefers to bury under material comfort
and propriety. A person like Haze Mote's grandfather, for example, who drives into Eastrod "as if he were just in time to

25. *Ibid.,* p. 390.
26. "Kierkegaard and Hamlet: Two Danish Princes," *The Anchor Review,*
No. 1, ed. Melvin J. Lasky (New York, 1955), p. 113.

save them all from Hell," is ludicrous but eminently useful to her theme.[27] The shouting old man may be dismissed as frenzied, exclamatory, unrestrained, and foolish, and yet his words are the truth which Miss O'Connor wants to present. The necessarily indirect methods of literature become even more elusive when Miss O'Connor develops her theme through characters whose clotted minds and emotions are repulsive, but she shows again and again that the violence of their action reflects a restlessness, a divine madness, which can be satisfied only with God.

Miss O'Connor best dramatizes the peculiar agonies of the possessed personality in Haze Motes, the street preacher in *Wise Blood*, and in Francis Marion Tarwater, the fourteen-year-old boy called to prophesy in *The Violent Bear It Away*. Plagued by an inverted Calvinistic conscience, Haze has come to the conclusion that Jesus is the cause of sin; therefore, he will avoid Jesus. Consequently, he preaches the Church Without Christ, "where the blind don't see and the lame don't walk and what's dead stays that way."[28] His passage from the rejection of the faith offered him in his childhood through self-inflicted mutilations to a final peace is a series of violent events leading him against his conscious will. Through blasphemy, seduction, and murder, Haze pursues the truth which he insists lies only in what he can see. At last, however, he blinds himself and in the darkness faces God. When he puts rocks and broken glass in the bottom of his shoes and binds barbed wire around his chest, his landlady points to the obvious conclusion, "You must believe in Jesus or you wouldn't do these foolish things."[29] Stifled by the bigoted fundamentalism of his mother's religion, stubborn in his ignorance and narrow-mindedness, and horrible in his violence, Haze Motes is as unattractive as Miss O'Connor could make him; nonetheless he is overtaken by God. The contrast be-

27. *Wise Blood* (New York: Harcourt, Brace and Company, 1952), p. 21.
28. *Ibid.*, p. 105.
29. *Ibid.*, p. 225.

tween the violence of Haze's rebellion and its resolution at his death into a stern but apparently tranquil faith is essential to the power of Miss O'Connor's presentation of man's need and God's omnipotence. Haze in his primitive ruthlessness is human nature as savage and perverse as Warren images it in *Brother to Dragons,* but redeemed in spite of itself.

Violence plays a similar part in the attempt of young Tarwater to escape the vocation of prophet. In *The Violent Bear It Away* the narrative is complicated by shifts in time when at relevant moments the past is brought in to explain the conflicts and reactions of characters. Fearful manifestations of God are present in the insane and self-righteous Uncle Mason and in the feeble-minded child Bishop, who looks like "the old man grown backwards to the lowest form of innocence."[30] The split within young Tarwater's personality between the godly and the satanic is voiced as an internal debate between the boy and a stranger. By using a child as the central figure Miss O'Connor suggests that the religious experience has nothing to do with time and age; in addition, the child's involvement makes the violence of religious possession all the more terrifying.

The stages of Tarwater's resistance and submission to his great-uncle's vision are marked by violence. Reared by his uncle to be a prophet, Tarwater first rebels by getting drunk and burning down the house instead of decently burying the old man. Like Haze, he attempts to exorcise the influence of religion by acts of violence which culminate in murder. The baptismal drowning of Bishop is both a symbolic killing of the old man and a pledge to the future. Unsatisfiable hunger and thirst make Tarwater's walk back to his home clearing a feverish torture. During the ride with the pale young man (the devil) who picks him up, he proudly announces his independence, but is drugged and raped. Finally he sees the burning tree which flares up out of the forest fire he has set as the ac-

30. *The Violent Bear It Away,* p. 111.

ceptable sign. He will return to the city to prophesy. He thus becomes another in the long line of prophets whose violence sustains the Kingdom of Heaven.

The ways of predicting and controlling violent human behavior which the twentieth century has learned, such as sociological and psychological engineering, never succeed in Miss O'Connor's fiction. The artist in "The Enduring Chill" who comes home to die finds his rationalistic defenses overthrown by the Holy Ghost.[31] Tom Shiftlet knows that the Atlanta doctor who held a human heart in his hand really understands nothing about it. Several characters mistake their knowledge of psychology, chemistry, and biology for infinite knowledge. Conspicuously, Sheppard, the city recreational director in "The Lame Shall Enter First," explains the destructiveness of the young delinquent Rufus Johnson in terms of the boy's compensating for his club foot and his deprived childhood. All Sheppard need do to rescue Rufus he believes is to express patience, understanding, and kindness, reasonable virtues which Sheppard discovers have little relation to the love grounded in justice and truth which the boy requires. Rufus scorns Sheppard's explanations because they ignore Satan, who really holds both man and boy in his power. When Sheppard's own young son protests that his father is good, Rufus hisses, "I don't care if he's good or not. He ain't right!"[32] The devil that Rufus never doubts is the same devil that the writer Thomas in "The Comforts of Home" discovers within himself when he resists his mother's attempts to help the nymphomaniac Star Drake. Rufus wrecks houses and Thomas shoots his mother, violent acts which demonstrate the reality of evil and by implication the reality of good.

Another of the mistaken, single-track rationalists is Rayber, Mason Tarwater's nephew, who believes that by his will pow-

31. "The Enduring Chill," *Harper's Bazaar*, XCII (July, 1958), 44-45, 94-108 *passim*.
32. "The Lame Shall Enter First," *Sewanee Review*, LXX (Summer, 1962), 348.

er and knowledge of facts he has freed himself from the obsessions of the old man. But at the sight of his dim-witted child, Rayber can be overwhelmed by a flood of irrational love, which Uncle Mason would never have hesitated to call divine. Under its spell, Rayber longs to see again the old man's eyes—"insane, fish-coloured, violent with their impossible vision of a world transfigured."[33] The only explanation which the non-believing Rayber can give for such a manifestation is the Gothic mystique of tainted blood. He feels that his family carries a mad religious enthusiasm as if its blood flowed from "some desert prophet or polesitter."[34]

These men of reason suggest that anything beyond the reaches of human logic and quantitative verification not only offends the modern intellect but also frightens it. Both Tarwater and his old uncle reject Rayber's desire to use them as the objects of psychological analysis, insisting instead on the sanctity of their individuality irreducible to statistics. The violent experiences of Miss O'Connor's people whether of love or of hate refute the possibility that human nature can be encompassed by man's ability to measure and to calculate. It is always the unaccountable which astonishes and compels them.

For those who are certain that cleanliness, hard work, and respectability betoken religious merit, there is a similar kind of shock. Human beings cannot impose their terms upon God. The "first," however, are seldom prepared to believe that they shall be "last." In "Revelation" Mrs. Ruby Turpin, pleased that Jesus has given her "a little of everything," voices her self-satisfaction to others waiting for the doctor to tend their ulcers and colds. She has a good husband; they own a farm just large enough for them to manage; they keep their hogs in a sanitary concrete pig parlor; they love the niggers who pick cotton for them. But the peculiar glare of the adolescent re-

33. *The Violent Bear It Away*, p. 114.
34. *Ibid.*

vealingly named Mary Grace ruffles Mrs. Turpin. Finally the
disturbed girl springs on Mrs. Turpin, who recognizes in the
attack something more than the violence of a deranged girl.
There is a message in the girl's whisper, "Go back to hell where
you came from, you old wart hog."[35] By the end of the day
the implications of the words have destroyed Mrs. Turpin's
complacency, and the woman who has been proud that she is
neither white trash nor nigger accuses Heaven of playing false
with her. The answer is a vision of souls thronging across the
fiery sky led by white trash, niggers, freaks, and lunatics. At
the end of the procession come the good people like the Turpins, still orderly, but Ruby "could see by their shocked and
altered faces that even their virtues were being burned
away."[36] The revelation is unmistakable. Its explicitness is
in keeping with the minds of the Ruby Turpins. And although
Mary Grace is a manipulated character, she expresses Miss
O'Connor's certainty that man can never dictate the conditions in which truth will be revealed. Because human defini-
tions of God's ways are too limited to be wholly accurate, they
must often be corrected by violence which disturbs the creature so that he may be open to the creator.

At times Miss O'Connor provides a counterpoint to the fictional events in an act which is grotesque without being violent, a Gothic restatement of the violence. When his Uncle
dies at the breakfast table, Tarwater continues to eat his
breakfast under the sightless eyes. The boy's defiance of the
corpse's claim to burial is his first active rebellion against
the tyranny under which he has lived. The knowing blood of
Enoch Emory is even more primitive than Haze Motes's. It
responds to Haze as a charismatic leader and forces Enoch to
steal a mummy from the museum to serve as the new Jesus.
For a short time something like the crude performance of a
Black Mass satisfies Enoch, but his regressive instinct leads

35. "Revelation," *The Sewanee Review*, LXXII (Spring, 1964), 192.
36. *Ibid.*, p. 201.

him to steal a gorilla costume and plunge through the woods disguised in this common parody of his origin. Instead of being merely subhuman, Enoch reverts to a prehuman state. All the gears of evolution seem thrown into reverse by such bizarre behavior. The grotesqueness suggests not merely that man may be dehumanized by his instincts but that unaltered wildness lies at his center.

A brisk current of humor, it has been noted, runs through Miss O'Connor's fiction, generally as an accompaniment to the violence and grotesqueness rather than as a theme deriving directly from these elements as it may in Faulkner and Caldwell. Regional idiom and custom quickly establish context and individualize characters, and lighten the grimness of the life Miss O'Connor views. Before setting out for Florida, the grandmother in "A Good Man Is Hard to Find," who is certain of her identity, dresses primly, so that in case of an accident she will be recognized as a lady. Tarwater has been properly educated, his uncle having taught him "Figures, Reading, Writing, and History beginning with Adam expelled from the Garden and going on down through the presidents to Herbert Hoover and on in speculation toward the Second Coming and the Day of Judgment."[37] Miss O'Connor has an exceptionally accurate ear for folk speech. The nasal Georgia and Tennessee hill country voices rise and fall in a cadence which is instantly identifiable and amusing in its flatness. Mrs. Shortley explaining the term "displaced person" to a Negro workman says, "It means they ain't where they were born at and there's nowhere for them to go—like if you was run out of here and wouldn't nobody have you."[38] In addition, the meeting of innocence and sophistication provokes humor when Miss O'Connor brings her isolated rural innocents, ignorant of modern gadgetry, into the city. Haze Motes looking for a used car to be his church and home is easily duped

37. *The Violent Bear It Away*, p. 4.
38. "The Displaced Person," *A Good Man Is Hard to Find*, p. 203.

by the salesman. The juxtaposition of the banal and the tragic, such as The Misfit's elaborate courtesy to his victims as they are called off to be shot, entertains by incongruity. Because the humor is kept entirely within the idiom of the characters, it never breaks the tone.

By the violence in her fiction Miss O'Connor scorns the "life-adjustment" philosophy of the twentieth century. The letter of the columnist to Sabbath Hawks mocks this theory of ease and conformity:

> . . . your real problem is one of adjustment to the modern world. Perhaps you ought to re-examine your religious values to see if they meet your needs in Life. A religious experience can be a beautiful addition to living if you put it in the proper prespective and do not let it warf you.[39]

These statements summarize precisely the attitude which Miss O'Connor attacks. In order to counter the state of mind which values temporizing as the chief virtue, she works with violence as a matter of fact, not as the point of departure for fantasy. The turmoil within her characters and their destructive relations with others occur as actualities, not as consequences of imaginative displacement. If the main characters seem "isolated from the general human context," as Donald Davidson believes, Miss O'Connor intends the reader to question that context as well as the characters.[40] The Southern milieu is a convenience to make articulate the moral hazards of all contemporary life. If the outlandishness of the characters nullifies the empathic identification which a reader might make with them, the bold lines of their portraiture nevertheless converge directly on the spiritual errors of the present, failings far more consequential than disruptive social changes or a malfunctioning economy. When these lines are too direct, the fiction lapses into preaching. The penultimate paragraph of "The Artificial Nigger," for example, slips into exegesis rather than narration, but in Miss O'Connor's fiction as a

39. *Wise Blood*, p. 119.
40. "A Prophet Went Forth" (review of *The Violent Bear It Away*) *New York Times Book Review*, Feb. 28, 1960, p. 4.

whole the demands of the story as story are the first to be satisfied.

The concentration with which Miss O'Connor writes accounts for much of her power. She rigorously excludes irrelevant details. Her economical, taut prose drives to its point without hesitation. The speed in the opening of her novel in progress illustrates her ability to develop tension swiftly:

Tilman had had his stroke in the state capital where he had gone on business, and he had stayed two weeks in the hospital there. He did not remember his arrival home by ambulance but his wife did. She had sat for two hours on the jump seat at his feet, gazing fixedly at his face. Only his left eye, twisted inward, seemed to harbor his former personality. It burned with rage. The rest of his face was prepared for death. Justice was grim and she took satisfaction in it when she found it. It might take just this ruin to wake Walter up.[41]

A sense of the inexorable permeates the style and the subject. Miss O'Connor refuses to make the compromise which she thinks some readers of contemporary literature demand, that is, "to separate mystery from manners and judgment from vision, in order to produce something a little more palatable to the modern temper."[42]

In this spirit, she uses violence to stress the urgency of the problem which she explores, to recall to a complacent world the radical alterations which faith makes in man's life, and to illustrate the despair which its denial brings. She displays the panic, frenzy, rage, and hypocrisy of the human outcast. His struggle to become his real self is profoundly emotional in contrast to the intellectual combat waged by Robert Penn Warren's characters. He comes finally into redemption, not through a tidy psychological pattern such as Warren sets but through acquiesence to the mystery of God, which burns out self-will in order to replace it with Divine Will. Along the way, violence is not only what is seen but also a way of seeing and judging.

41. "Why Do the Heathens Rage?" *Esquire*, LX (July, 1963), 60.
42. "The Fiction Writer and His Country," p. 160.

III. Violence as revelation: Eudora Welty

The special province of Eudora Welty is the point at which the tangible, in the sense of the actual, and the intangible, in the sense of vision and interpretation, fuse. Violent and grotesque persons or situations arise in either component of Miss Welty's fiction. They may be reports from uncannily sharp observations of the action, or they may be illuminations of what the actual means. These elements do not represent merely a private attitude toward life, for they assist in a larger interpretation, fully objectified in fictional form, to which they are always subordinate. The subtly combined details are never ends in themselves. They are proportioned and balanced to declare that health resides within order and illness within disorder. Miss Welty enlarges experience by relating its nuances with precision and intensity. She sustains the fusion of the tangible and the intangible best in the short story form which demands concentration and control. The extra meaning which envelops the facts of the narratives tends to become diffused in a longer work, such as *Robber Bridegroom*. In a novel like *Delta Wedding* the fusion of elements is stabilized in symbols.

By superimposing the extraordinary on the ordinary, Miss Welty breaks through the commonplace to find unsuspected meaning. Squalid actuality may take on a glimmer of magic. In her introduction to Miss Welty's first collection of short stories, *A Curtain of Green and Other Stories* (1941), Katherine Anne Porter expressed particular admiration for the stories "where external act and the internal voiceless life of the human imagination almost meet and mingle on the mysterious threshold between dream and waking, one reality refusing to admit or confirm the existence of the other, yet both conspiring toward the same end."[1] This commingling has continued to be the achievement of Miss Welty's work. In *Robber Bridegroom*, a novella published in 1942, Miss Welty mixes the violence of frontier life along the Old Natchez Trace with the dream-violence of fairy tales and legends. The mood of *The Wide Net and Other Stories* (1943) is suggested by the opening phrase, "Whatever happened, it happened in extraordinary times, in a season of dreams. . . ."[2] This feeling carries over into *The Golden Apples* (1949), a collection of stories relating the growth of the young in Morgana, Mississippi, and into *The Bride of the Innisfallen* (1955), filled with tales of mythic journeys like that of the legendary Odysseus to and from Circe, or that of present-day Gabriella from New York to Naples. In the novel *Delta Wedding* (1946) and the novella *The Ponder Heart* (1954) Miss Welty delineates the conflicts and eccentricities of Southern families to reveal the polarity of human interdependence, the cruelty and the kindness inherent in every act.

Whatever enlargement of reality Miss Welty makes through violence, she begins with Southern life as strongly realized as it is in the work of her fellow Mississippian William Faulkner. A native of Jackson, Miss Welty has remained with her family there. While Faulkner in Yoknapatawpha County created a complex epitome of his idea of the South, Eudora Welty has seemed to embody her culture so fully within herself that the details which she selects automatically fall into patterns reflecting the whole. She considers this almost instinctive knowledge of local people and places essential equipment for a writer, for without it, she observes, there is "uncertainty about what the characters really think or mean, ambiguity about what they do or fail to do, or . . . queer hap-

---

1. *A Curtain of Green and Other Stories* (New York: Doubleday, Doran and Company, Inc., 1941), p. xxi.
2. "First Love," *The Wide Net and Other Stories* (New York: Harcourt, Brace and Company, 1943), p. 3.

hazardness in the novel's shape or form."[3] The exactness of locale in which Miss Welty's fiction is rooted protects it from the blurring of time and place even when fantasy takes over. It has also protected her from being excessively influenced by writers in a similar idiom like Faulkner. What is said and done rings with her own voice. With character and conversation, emotion and act, she evokes subtle states of being in which responses to experience are minutely identified and individualized. Whether Miss Welty is dealing with frustration, insanity, suicide, and murder, or with tenderness, patience, and pastoral calm, her precision is an antidote to depersonalization in the contemporary world. She reinstates feeling as a valid way of apprehending life and thus reassures the reader that he is a live, responsive being.

The most important emotional experience which Miss Welty illuminates is the privacy of the consciousness. The isolation and separation which Robert Penn Warren treats as a pathological condition she accepts as inherently dignified because it is the fundamental fact of human life, albeit a fact which involves men, women, and children in the capricious, the ridiculous, the violent, the sad, and the grotesque. The connection between violence and human isolation is viewed very differently by Robert Penn Warren and Eudora Welty. Warren considers violence the disastrous outcome of separateness; therefore, he creates violent incidents to identify this important source of catastrophe in man's life. Miss Welty, on the other hand, lets violence reveal to characters hitherto unaware of their condition the fact of their aloneness. In her work the confrontation vivifies the individual's sense of his existence and only rarely, and then obliquely, criticizes the social context of his life. By transcending the specifications which make a character and his experience palpably Southern, Miss Welty concentrates on the meaning of violence in general human experience. The destruction of a beautiful

3. "Place in Fiction," *South Atlantic Quarterly*, LV (Jan., 1956), 68.

white heron in "A Still Moment," for example, shocks the three men who meet on the Old Natchez Trace into a new understanding both of the distance between their inner selves and of the nature of the goals they espouse. Audubon must kill beauty before he can paint it; Lorenzo Dow, the frontier preacher lusting after souls, staggers before the realization that his concepts like Time and Separateness do not exist for God; the murderer Murrell suddenly doubts his faith that by killing other men he can solve the mystery of being. These three lives brought together for a moment quickly separate, but only after Miss Welty by an incident of violence has radically rearranged their content.

In a pair of stories, "The Hitch-hikers" and "Death of a Traveling Salesman," violence reveals the emptiness and dissatisfaction customarily kept hidden in the life of a typical American figure—the salesman. Miss Welty demonstrates the power of either external or internal violence to shake people free from their complacency and insensitivity. Tom Harris takes two hitchhikers, scarcely more than strangers to one another, into Dulcie, a small Delta town. This act is charged with unusual meaning when one of the riders kills the other out of exasperation for his "uppity" self-assurance. Harris follows his accustomed round of casual entertainment in the town, but the comfortless rain in the ugly town, the reminiscences of one of the party girls who had known him five years earlier, and the suspense of waiting for hospital reports on his fatally injured passenger force him to admit his condition:

. . . there had been other violence not of his doing—other fights, not quite so pointless, but fights in his car; fights, unheralded confessions, sudden lovemaking—none of any of this his, not his to keep, but belonging to the people of these towns he passed through, coming out of their rooted pasts and their mock rambles, coming out of their time. He himself had no time. He was free; helpless.[4]

In a region where there is time and a past this kind of un-

4. *A Curtain of Green,* p. 141.

relatedness constitutes a wilful choice of isolation and its consequent violence.

Again in "Death of a Traveling Salesman" violence is educative. Here it is completely internalized as the fears which disturb the salesman R. J. Bowman at the approach of death, and thus it becomes the whole texture of the story—the theme, the mood, and the agent of revelation. Bowman, apparently traveling again after a month of illness—"a life of fever and privacy"—lapses into delirium. Moving in the burning landscape of his feverish dreams he has a vision of a simple, idyllic, pastoral life shared by figures who are alternately mother and son, husband and wife. Closed out of their circle of love he shivers in recognition of the emptiness, futility, and unnaturalness of his life. Like Mr. Arcularis in Conrad Aiken's story of death, Bowman succumbs in full knowledge that he has never learned the secret of communication. Miss Welty brings her two salesmen to the same realization by exposing them through violence to the meaning of their choices. The impact of Bowman's discovery is more powerful than that of Harris because it is a full revelation of a state of mind.

The same intensity of emotional analysis characterizes a child's perception of isolation in "A Memory," and makes the recognitions shatteringly violent. The bathers whom the child watches seem to have become reconciled to anger and ugliness in their lives. In this acquiescence she senses a threat. Experience will always disorder her dream. She can love a boy at school so long as his consciousness makes no demands on her. But she is stricken with horror to realize that no amount of obsessive care on her part will protect her from the violence of the unexpected which she cannot control. To become an adult she must enter fully into the contingencies which threaten human life.

In most instances in Miss Welty's fiction, violence does not destroy the central character but corrects his view of himself. The fact that his consciousness is separate from all other consciousnesses is not altered by his new perception, but the separation no longer cripples him. Having recognized his condition, he may be enabled to communicate with others. Although his bridges between island consciousnesses are unsubstantial and need continuous rebuilding, he can now live without despair. If the character suffers from the antecedent condition of being himself one of the unaware, he may be awakened by violence. Once alert, he can turn his unawareness into awareness in the kind of conversion which Henry James celebrated as marking the person on whom nothing is lost.

Miss Welty occasionally underscores the separateness of human beings by violence in nature. Under ordinary conditions her land is somnolent, changing slowly from season to season. When beset by storm or flood, however, it subjects the occupants to primeval violence and emphasizes the tenuousness of their presence. In "At the Landing," the flooding Mississippi River cuts the characters off from their earth roots and sets them afloat in a new environment where old patterns of relationships no longer obtain. Violence is the basis of the new relationships into which Jenny enters to find herself. It is an equinoctial storm in "The Winds" which stirs the young Josie to contemplate the psychological distances in her life and to yearn to bring together in herself "all that was wild and beloved and estranged."[5] The unusual and brief violence of the storm matches the sudden insight given to Josie. Such incidents in which the violence of the natural world lays bare man's solitude are rare in Miss Welty's work, for generally the revelation occurs in the human dimension only.

The most complex human dimension for Miss Welty is the family. It has what she has called an essential nourishment for people as well as books, "a known set of standards to struggle within or against."[6] Its members, willingly or unwillingly, are rooted deep in their connections with others. The power of the family to hold lives together and to direct them has per-

5. *The Wide Net*, p. 139.
6. "Place in Fiction," p. 68.

sisted as a standard by which to judge the acts of individuals. Hodding Carter, for example, testifies, "I was raised to believe that whoever harmed my kinsman was also my enemy and whoever befriended him was friend of mine and that the closer the relationship the greater the obligations and the privilege to stand near."[7] Miss Welty's families are benevolently violent, chastising the wayward by words and keeping out the interloper by refusing him his identity. The Ponders of *The Ponder Heart* and the Fairchilds of *Delta Wedding* know who they are to the point of relishing their eccentricities and accepting their manners without question. Their certainty is their version of social order.

The order which the family in *Delta Wedding* represents, however, does not radiate outward to stabilize the surrounding community. In fact, the family is so tightly enclosed that it threatens violence to those who try to enter. Robbie, who is fighting to establish that she married George Fairchild, not his family, is warned by Troy Flavin, another outsider, that "it's a close family. . . . Too close, could be."[8] Nervous and high-strung, hypersensitive to one another, the Fairchilds nevertheless have "secret, despiting ways to happiness."[9] The tension between taking for the self and giving for the clan is incipiently violent. It accounts for the apparently unmotivated turns and tides in the emotional currents in *Delta Wedding*. Miss Welty perceives that the private claims of the family are finally destructive unless balanced by public obligations. The most vital Fairchild and the most puzzling one to his family is George because his love encompasses the world as well as his family. Such inclusive love invalidates the false pride of the other members of the family. The characters who are able to see through the violence and pretensions of the Fairchilds are the two women who attach themselves to

7. *Where Main Street Meets the River* (New York: Rinehart and Company, Inc., 1952), p. 10.
8. *Delta Wedding* (New York: Harcourt, Brace and Company, 1955), p. 141.
9. *Ibid.*, p. 74.

George—his wife Robbie and his cousin Laura. Symbolically Miss Welty makes clear that the family gives strength and order to the South only when it includes rather than excludes. Laura belongs to the family when at the end of the novel she stands with arms outstretched toward the falling stars, a link between the clan and the world. Then there is radiance and reassurance.

Physical defects and grotesque behavior under Miss Welty's subtle manipulation depict not only human isolation but also a pride in that privacy as a condition which distinguishes the individual from the mass. Although the deaf boy Joel in "First Love" is cut off from any expression of the love he feels for Aaron Burr, who conspires at the inn where Joel blacks boots, the boy knows more about Burr's life than do those who have unimpaired faculties. Ellie and Albert Morgan in "The Key" are trapped by their deaf-muteness into a marriage which they hope will become happy when they reach Niagara Falls. As deaf-mutes they are, by a natural defect, separated from those who speak and hear, but another kind of distance is essential. By means of the key which Albert finds and cherishes, Miss Welty sensitively indicates that he wishes to be set apart from his wife, to enjoy "the secret and proper separation that lies between a man and a woman. . . ."[10] The elderly Mr. Marblehall believes he has solved the mystery of human behavior by duplicity. In one part of Natchez he has an ancestral home, a wife, and a son; across town he lives with another wife and another son, arrangements all accomplished since he became sixty. He feeds on horror magazines, hugging to himself the feeling that he, too, could shock the town by revealing his career. In "Powerhouse" almost uninterrupted description of the monstrous Negro jazz musician emphasizes the obscene motion, the sweating fat, the drumming of the piano which distinguish him as a primitive force. Whether keyed to violence or to grotesqueness, the mood of each story is individual with characters and situations sharp-

10. *A Curtain of Green*, p. 71.

ly differentiated, for in her writing Miss Welty illustrates
Pascal's aphorism that "the greater intellect one has, the more
originality one finds in men. Ordinary persons find no difference between men."[11]

A character's pride in his individuality, however, may become vulgar and ludicrous as the grotesqueness of "Petrified
Man" and "Why I Live at the P. O." demonstrate. The gossip
of Leota and her customer in a small town beauty shop epitomizes the idle curiosity, mindlessness, crudity, sensation-
seeking, and avarice of humankind. The idea of beauty as
something to be dispensed by Leota amid hairnets, shampoo,
stale peanuts, and a whining drawl is in itself a grotesque
jangling of whatever overtones of the ideal the term *beauty*
might convey. Leota's glibness and crassness, caught up at
the moment in the pleasure of describing the freaks of a traveling show, are undone by her renter, Mrs. Pike, who identifies
the petrified man in the show as the person wanted for the
rape of four women, and collects the reward. The vulgar
superstructure of superiority which Leota has built is a skele-
ton of the petrification—intellectual, aesthetic, and moral—of
a world which has no challenge except the one flung out by
Mrs. Pike's Billy Boy, who has been underfoot during the entire story: "If you're so smart, why ain't you rich?"[12]

The paranoiac postmistress in "Why I live at the P. O." reveals her persecution complex and the single-track simplicities of her family in an amusing rattle of indignation. The
Fourth of July in China Grove, Mississippi, sizzles with the
violence of family conflict: Papa Daddy sulks over the suggestion that he should cut off his beard, Uncle Rondo drunk-
enly parades into the front yard in Stella-Rondo's negligee and
tosses firecrackers into the narrator's bedroom, Stella-Rondo
has "conniption fits" at the suggestion that the allegedly
adopted child she has brought home is her own. But the post-

11. *Pensées,* trans. William Finlayson Trotter (London: J. M. Dent and
Sons, Ltd., 1931), p. 4.
12. *A Curtain of Green,* p. 52.

mistress settles everything by moving into the post office. "There I was with the whole entire house on Stella-Rondo's side and turned against me," she explains. "If I have anything at all I have pride."[13] The uncontrived humor of the postmistress' speech pattern is a microcosmic reflection of the niggling frustration, the irritations, the repressions of provincial life which self-delusion can enlarge into a rebellion, comic to the reader but righteous to the instigator. In this kind of portrayal Miss Welty domesticates violence and makes it appear a constant element of daily life.

Much of the violent and abnormal behavior of Miss Welty's characters stems from insanity, the collapse of the individual in a society, or more specifically, in a family oblivious of his need to be loved and believed in. Women most frequently are the victims, although some of them like Clytie in the story of her name have brothers and fathers who are also deranged. Despised or ignored by their families and friends, these characters sink into a confusion which Miss Welty turns into an elegy for love. Across the lament there then falls an anti-elegiac note of violence which expresses the agony of insanity. Clytie, for example, searches each face for the sign of beauty and communication that would answer her craving for companionship, and when she sees the reflection of her own suffering face in the water of the rain barrel, she sinks toward it and drowns.

The insanity and resulting violence of three of the women in Miss Welty's stories is the product of sexual frustration. Their violence is pathetic rather than tragic, and in only one instance does the private abnormality represent the failure of a society. When Miss Eckhart in "June Recital" transfers her thwarted dreams to Virgie Rainey, her most talented music pupil, disaster follows. Virgie's refusål to live vicariously for her teacher, although a decision necessary for her own life, is the cruelty which destroys Miss Eckhart. The mental decline of Miss Eckhart, culminating in her setting fire to the

13. *Ibid.*, p. 103.

house where she had once lived and in being rejected a second time by Virgie, not only hardens Virgie's selfishness but also introduces the spectator children Cassie and Loch Morrison to the misery of the adult world. Another seemingly proper woman, Miss Sabina in "Asphodel," explodes into violence when her husband is unfaithful. She whips him from the house, subdues the townspeople with her demonic energy, and finally destroys the post office because in her possessed mind letters mean lovers. The only loss which the insane Miss Myra in "The Burning" regrets when Sherman's men burn her home is that of Phinny, the mulatto child of her brother whom she claims for her own. Her sister Miss Theo with the help of their Negro servant hangs Miss Myra and herself. The dead women fall like emblems of the ruined South while the Negro robs them and hurries toward the liberating army. The story is free from malice, as if Miss Welty could meditate on the destruction of her region without sentimentalizing either its womanhood or its slaves. If the Negro appears as a thief, the white aristocrat appears exhausted, corrupted, and demented, competent only to commit suicide. This story is a rare instance in which Miss Welty turns violence into an explicit comment on the Southern past.

In stories which involve afflicted or dispossessed persons, Miss Welty often achieves a reversal whereby the afflicted instruct the apparently normal. The blind lead the seeing, whose sight, it turns out, cannot penetrate spiritual darkness. As Eunice Glenn points out, "Those who are seemingly defenseless become superior; while those who are tangibly superior become the really unfortunate, because of a more important deficiency within themselves."[14] The three ladies who try to manage the life of feeble-minded Lily Daw illustrate this principle. Suddenly responding to the normality of the girl's desire to get married, they take her off the train for Ellisville and the Institute for the Feeble-Minded and rush

14. "Fantasy in the Fiction of Eudora Welty," *A Southern Vanguard: The John Peale Bishop Memorial Volume*, ed. Allen Tate (New York: Prentice-Hall, Inc., 1947), p. 80.

her into the arms of the deaf xylophone player who had asked
for her. Accepting Lily's view as normal is easier for the ladies
than bearing the guilt of putting her in an institution. Lily
Daw's only role is to wait bovinely placid while the ladies
flutter between solutions and finally come around to her
choice. Thus out of the timidity of the normal intelligences,
the dim-witted Lily Daw wins. Here the reversal is a joke on
the narrow-minded presumptuousness of the human race.

The reversal in "Keela, the Outcast Indian Maiden," on the
other hand, is a moral achievement reached through the suffering of the Negro dwarf, Little Lee Roy. Forced to join a
circus, he had been billed as a wild Indian maiden who ate live
chickens. The treatment which he received is so painful that
Miss Welty has explained that the story is the only actual one
she ever used, for "it was too horrible to make up."[15] Enduring loathsome indignities has freed Little Lee Roy from the
necessity of feeling justice or injustice, but his experience has
imprisoned Steve, the young white sideshow barker, in a tor-
ment of guilt. Steve and the spectators had accepted the
performance as reality until one person, independent and
sympathetic enough to ask questions, stopped the hideous exploitation. Now that Steve wants to do penance for his complicity as the person who lured others into the show, the Negro
is strangely remote and inaccessible. Through the grotesqueness of this experience Miss Welty exposes one of the weaknesses by which human beings comfort themselves—the hope
of a second chance. There are relationships, she implacably
demonstrates, which—although blundered into by the innocent—are too monstrous to be rectified.

Miss Welty has sometimes been criticized for not writing
more often about the "Negro problem." It is, of course, spe-
cious to insist that a writer occupy himself with particular
social issues no matter how meritorious their consideration
might be. He knows his own talent well enough to refuse ex-

15. Robert Van Gelder, "An Interview with Eudora Welty," *Writers and Writing* (New York: Charles Scribner's Sons, 1946), p. 289.

ternal, though well-meaning directives. That Miss Welty is sensitive to racial injustice is clear from the story of Keela. That she is profoundly moved by current racial violence is evident in her most recent story "Where Is the Voice Coming From?" Here she is reacting almost instantaneously to the murder of Medgar Evers, and she wisely chooses to imagine the mind of the white murderer rather than that of the Negro. What the white man narrates is not a complex account of someone who felt ancient blood antipathies, or a desire to make the South safe for white supremacy, or a compulsion to exorcise his heritage of racial guilt. He killed because he was hot and tired and bored: "I done what I done for my own pure-D satisfaction."[16] The voice whines about Negroes who speak on television, Negro children who are arrested in demonstrations, and the Negro who has a paved roadway and green grass as if these were the petty annoyances of insects on a steamy night. In killing Roland Summers, the narrator has merely slapped a particularly persistent mosquito. This undramatic recital of violence opens a pit into which the reader stares, confronted by the reality that the private refusal to think of any man as a human being is a public hell. Because it is the consistent tone of the voice which delivers the indictment of the violence and the attitude which produces it, the intrusion of the wife weakens the intensity of the story. The two pages of the story, however, are compact with the keen articulation of a state of mind in which violence is utterly damning because the act and the judgment upon it cannot be connected.

By shifting into the realm of fantasy in other stories, Miss Welty can manipulate violence and grotesqueness with utmost freedom because they are no longer tied to the literal. She makes fantasy a method of organization and interpretation rather than content. The later volumes of Miss Welty's short stories, such as *The Golden Apples* and *The Bride of the*

16. "Where Is the Voice Coming From?" *The New Yorker,* XXIX (July 6, 1963), 24-25.

Innisfallen, are permeated by the improbable and the imaginary. Stories which begin in some distortion of human relations incubate in an imagination which forces every element to yield its hidden significance. Miss Welty does not impose meaning from esoteric private sources, nor does she intrude commentary; instead, she works in her material until it takes on the universality of myth and dream. The transformation is from action to slow motion, for as states of mind are emphasized, violence subsides into imagined activity. The character moves in the actual world only enough to sustain physical life; his real life is interior. It is as vivid and compelling as a dream, and like a dream, it has its own set of rules. These permit distortions and excesses which in the daily world would be disbelieved. Here they cast light into corners of loves and hates, hopes and fears ordinarily left dark. The odd or the strange or the gruesome are means of exploration, not an end as they appear in Caldwell's fiction. Their discoveries tell much about the inner and inarticulate life of man.

By the fantasies of the MacLain twins in *The Golden Apples,* for example, Miss Welty portrays the despairing search of modern man for joy. The violence may be entirely internal as it is in the story "The Whole World Knows." The murderous frustration which Ran MacLain feels toward his unfaithful wife would never be suspected by Morgana citizens, who treat the rupture as a lover's quarrel soon to be mended. But in three bursts of imagined violence, Miss Welty reveals how deeply Ran has been wounded. In his mind he crushes his rival with a croquet mallet when he hears the phrase, "You're dead on Woody"; while his wife mends his shirt, he shoots her; in a tourist cabin with the country girl Maideen he shoots himself. Ironically it is Maideen who in another story is reported as having actually committed suicide. The violence of Ran's internal life gives his estrangement from his wife, which reflects his prior estrangement from his father, a seriousness which the onlookers would deny.

In "Music from Spain" violence triggers the interior excitement which for a day releases middle-aged Eugene MacLain —prototype of the world's "little men"—from his humdrum existence. Without warning he slaps his wife at breakfast. This protest and the realization of the inglorious transience of life, which comes when he sees a woman killed by a trolley, prepare him for escape with his uninhibited alter ego, a Spanish musician. Eugene's desires for self-gratification and for self-destruction are acted out in the Spaniard's gargantuan eating and in his seeming threat to hurl Eugene over the cliff. A glimpse of grotesqueness allows the author swiftly to indicate the transformation which a sense of freedom works in Eugene. A woman strangely birthmarked appears beautiful to him. Miss Welty's brief description illustrates how quickly she can move from precise details to fanciful comment and yet keep all in the mood of the observing character:

Curves, scrolls, dark brown areas on light brown, were beautifully placed on her body, as if by design, with pools about the eyes, at the nape of her neck, at the wrist, and about her legs, too, like fawn spots, visible through her stockings. She had the look of waiting in leafy shade.[17]

These violent and grotesque expressions of Eugene's unconsciousness or semi-consciousness do not bring him joy, but they do reconcile the warring parts of his nature and restore him to a measure of integrity.

Miss Welty achieves one of her subtlest effects with violence when she glides into the treatment of a universal theme, such as love and the inviolate consciousness, by means of myths which man has devised to explain his hurt to himself. In "At the Landing," the Negro cabins, the officious women of the neighborhood, and the sleepy haze which envelops the settlement forecast an ordinary earthbound life for Jenny, but Billy Floyd intrudes with the primordial violence of a field and river god. He violates Jenny. She then becomes a kind of earth

17. *The Golden Apples* (New York: Harcourt, Brace and Company, 1949), p. 174.

goddess doomed to wander in search of Floyd and to accept
the violations of the men she meets on the way, knowing that
"the secrecy of life was the terror of it."[18]

Similar echoes from Miss Welty's attentive reading of myths
and legends, folklore and fairy tales sound in such stories as
"Asphodel," "Livvie," "Shower of Gold," and "The Wide Net,"
and particularly in the novella *The Robber Bridegroom*. This
material affords her a formal pattern into which violence,
grotesqueness, and psychological instability may be fitted
with meaning. "Asphodel" is an account of a Southern lady's
betrayal and violent defiance pictured in scenes like a frieze
on a Grecian urn. The three old maids disport themselves like
nymphs at the ruins of the house belonging to Mr. Don
McInnis, Miss Sabina's husband. They recite the violence of
Miss Sabina's life. A satyr-like figure which they take for Mr.
McInnis appears, and they flee, pursued by a flock of goats.
The mingling of the classical and the modern gives the frustrations of the women style and significance impossible to
attain at a purely factual level.

Dragging the river for William Wallace's wife in "The Wide
Net" is a chthonian festival. Men and boys from the village
endanger themselves, beat off a stranger who comes into their
territory, frolic at a fish fry, see the King of the Snakes undu-
late through the water, and weather a fierce storm. They return like warriors, and William Wallace fights to prove that
he is supreme. His heroics end in the discovery that his wife
is safe at home. But nothing has been wasted, for the males
have proved themselves and have propitiated the river. In
such stories the twisting of commonplace reality by ritualistic
action and by mythic characters and situations renders everything timeless. Violence as part of this Olympian elevation is
an enlarged dramatic gesture like the movement of a Greek
actor to make himself visible. It draws attention to the meaning of the act, not to the act itself. Like the enlargements in

18. *The Wide Net,* p. 189.

Greek drama, the distortions which Miss Welty thus uses ultimately suggest not the transient distress of life but its endless heroism.

The Robber Bridegroom is Miss Welty's most comprehensive amalgam of fantasy in which Grimm's fairy tales, Greek myth, Biblical story, and Mississippi folklore are mixed. In this book, violence and grotesquerie form a whimsical allegory of the chief experiences in man's life—self-recognition, love, and hate; and a brief recapitulation of dynamic phases of American history—westward expansion, economic exploitation, and urbanization. The equivalencies, however, are never made exact and clear.

The foreboding forests along the Old Natchez Trace, where Indians capture and torture travelers and where gigantic alligators swallow horsemen, are the dark wood in which Rosamond hunts for an understanding of herself. She is robbed of love by the bandit-gentleman Jamie Lockhart in a Cupid-Psyche relationship. When Rosamond and Jamie are reunited, they become the first buorgeois couple in the history of fairy tales. They live in a marble and cypress house on Lake Pontchartrain, and for Jamie "the outward change from bandit to merchant had been almost too easy to count it a change at all, and he was enjoying all the same success he had ever had."[19] Here the playful tone of the sly social commentary as well as the fairy tale quality makes the violent elements amusing.

Pioneer life along the Natchez Trace was generically violent. Rosamond's father, a pastoral innocent, meditates on the violence of the Southern frontier. He recalls murder, banditry, slave selling, and lynching. In the silence of the wild land "massacre is hard to tell from the performance of other rites."[20] But this land finally will take all the human lives set down in it, from the Indian and the white hunter to the planter and

19. *The Robber Bridegroom* (New York: Doubleday, Doran and Company, Inc., 1942), pp. 184-185.
20. *Ibid.*, p. 143.

the merchant. It seems to have the power of revenge which Faulkner invokes in his hunting stories.

Violence which exists wholly in language is a source of humor particularly in Miss Welty's stories of families, such as *Delta Wedding* and *The Ponder Heart*. None of the characters have the incantatory power of Mr. Gant and Eugene or the cadence of Faulkner's narrative voice, but the violence of their speech suggests that they take a pleasure in hyperbole, which observers like Wilbur J. Cash have identified as part of the South's romanticism. With Miss Welty's characters, the threat to kill others is an expression both of affection and of irritation. Battle Fairchild tells his children they will have to kill or whip their mother to make her rest, speaking, as the author says, "in the exasperation and helplessness of much love."[21] Disgusted that the plantation overseer Troy Flavin is going to marry a Fairchild daughter, Aunt Mac thinks of drowning him in a bayou, and Tempe would pull out the eyes of Robbie, who had rashly left her Fairchild husband. Such exclamations, trivial in themselves, help to establish the atmosphere of domestic babble and conflict which surrounds the characters. They belong to a verbal tradition which children learn from their elders and which outsiders rarely learn.

Confusion about the meaning of this tradition makes the trial of Uncle Daniel Ponder a comic opera. The case for the prosecution of weak-minded Uncle Daniel for the alleged murder of his young wife hinges on his message to her: "I'm going to kill you dead, Miss Bonnie Dee, if you don't take me back."[22] Uncle Daniel's niece, Miss Edna Earle, narrates the story in injured tones intended just as unmistakably to identify her as a lady as does the bunch of violets pinned to the grandmother in Flannery O'Connor's "A Good Man Is Hard to Find." The county attorney persists in misunderstanding the language habits of the region until the court-

21. *Delta Wedding,* p. 20.
22. *The Ponder Heart* (New York: Harcourt, Brace and Company, 1954), p. 110.

room is reduced to bedlam. Edna Earle explains, "It's all in a way of speaking. . . . With some people, it's little threats. With others it's liable to be poems."[23] Miss Welty catches the importance of verbal violence in a society largely held together by oral communication, and proves that no statement is accepted for its content but rather for its intention.

In keeping with her theory that the private consciousness merits respectful consideration and understanding no matter how extreme the manifestations of individuality may be, Miss Welty invents a notable variety of people and situations to illustrate her view. The theme of love and separateness, which Robert Penn Warren admirably analyzed when her fiction first began to appear, characterizes her work. This duality of closeness and distance, inclusion and exclusion, sharing and withdrawing, union and disjunction provides for her meditation the subject which she calls the "pervading and changing mystery" of relationship. "Brutal or lovely," she adds, "the mystery waits for people wherever they go, whatever extreme they run to."[24]

In this context, violence may simply be illustrations of the isolation of the consciousness or it may represent the effort to come into a relationship with another consciousness. But Miss Welty's singular gift in the use of this element is to make it part of the inner logic of the story which works a genuine change in a character's perception of his condition. Although their lives may be filled with loneliness, frustration, and even baseness, the characters are never victims as are Caldwell's grotesques nor are they bathetically non-heroic. Without declaiming, Miss Welty insists on the validity of each person, even when he is absurdly irrational. Violence and grotesqueness, then, never overwhelm her characters, but in the end become part of her affirmation of their distinctiveness and their merit.

When Miss Welty translates the mundane into fantasy, she

23. *Ibid.*, p. 117.
24. "How I Write," *Virginia Quarterly Review*, XXXI (Spring, 1955), 250.

takes violence and grotesqueness into a new dimension where they are controlled by the needs of the states of mind which she wishes to portray. These few magic inches from the commonplace enable her, as they enabled Hawthorne, to make articulate psychological events which a strict realist could never chronicle. Distortions become symbolic of the struggle to convert disorder, misery, and deception into order, joy, and truth. The South, like Hawthorne's New England, furnishes her the necessary security of place with its characteristic tones of speech, social assumptions, tempo of daily life, and patterns of behavior from which to leap into the unacknowledged or the unexplored interior world of each human mind. As Miss Welty has said of Faulkner and Lawrence, ". . . we enter the magic world of pure sense, of evocation—the shortest cut known through the woods."[25]

IV. The cost of freedom: William Styron

The conditions of freedom for man within institutions and within himself occupy William Styron. Whether rebelling against oppressive authority or craving the direction of kindly authority, his characters are trying to establish a creative relation between freedom and discipline. Their attempts bring them up against violence in major manifestations. Each of Styron's novels counts the cost of this pursuit in terms of frustration, jealously, betrayal, despair, and death.

In his first novel, *Lie Down in Darkness* (1951) Styron records the decline of freedom and the increase of violence during the dissolution of a present-day Virginia family. *The Long March,* a short novel published the following year, in-

25. "The Reading and Writing of Short Stories," *Atlantic Monthly,* CLXXXIII (March, 1949), 49.

dicts military authority through incidents of violence in a Marine camp in the Carolinas. His third and most ambitious novel, *Set This House on Fire* (1960), traces an artist's descent into the despair of profligacy and the emergence into hope and discipline.

The South which Styron uses is middle-class, urban, and contemporary. There is a strong sense that the only ideals and manners available to this world come from the past. Reflecting Styron's own recent residence in Europe, the action in *Set This House on Fire* occurs among Americans in Italy; but the South is present in the judgments which the narrator, a Virginian, makes on the violence. Styron was born in Newport News, Virginia, in 1925, and was educated at Christchurch in Virginia and at Duke University. A course in short story writing under Hiram Haydn at the New School for Social Research set him to writing seriously. His method he describes as working by instinct. "In the end," he believes, "you get some kind of poetic insight not possible if you work formalistically."[1]

In making the case for man's inner freedom, Styron in his first two novels begins from the outside. He examines the institutional frames which may fix the movement of a life. The initial nature of man as a creature with or without original sin, freedom of will, or rationality does not concern Styron as it does Robert Penn Warren and Flannery O'Connor. Instead, he looks at the circumstances of existence and describes their support or their destruction of the desires of man. Not until his third novel does Styron attempt a detailed explication of the state of mind of a single central character, and even here the antecedents for the action are not formulated as a theory of the nature of all men but as a description of the self-chosen defects of one man at one time.

Although *The Long March* is a classic instance of violence attendant upon the violation of individuality by the military, the urgency of the issue gains little from the Southern locale.

1. *Saturday Review of Literature*, XXXIV (Sept. 15, 1951), 12.

The setting is a convenience of fact and makes no particular contribution to the meaning of the novel. The greater power of *Lie Down in Darkness* and *Set This House on Fire* comes largely from their fuller development but also from the measurement of violence against the standards of established Southern manners and customs. *The Long March,* however, energetically protests the accretion of violence in the twentieth century and the deadening of conscience and sensibility which almost uninterrupted warfare has produced. Like Nicolas Berdyaev's *The Fate of Man in the Modern World,* it speaks against the morality of continuous war according to which "man may be used in any way desired for the attainment of inhuman or anti-human aims."[2]

Styron's charge against the military mind centers in the protest of Captain Mannix of the United States Marine Corps Reserve against a thirty-six-mile forced march ordered by Colonel Templeton of the regulars. The illogic of setting off on such a course merely to create new *esprit de corps* and to prove that the Battalion is not "doping off" arouses Mannix's contempt and fury. In order to protest, however, Mannix has to play his role in the system. By forcing himself and his company to complete the march, he defies Templeton, who expects the group to drop out. Styron's problem is to make the representatives of the civilian and of the military minds sufficiently complex to develop a convincing conflict. Instead of creating small preliminary incidents to dramatize the opposition of the two men, Styron depends chiefly upon the commentary of Lieutenant Culver, Mannix's friend. As a consequence of this method, the decisive encounter between the Colonel and the Captain near the end of the march when Mannix insults Templeton is less explosive than the author wants the reader to believe. The frustration which accumulates during the march points toward this collision, but face to face the two men say in four-letter words what has already

2. *The Fate of Man in the Modern World* (Ann Arbor: University of Michigan Press, Ann Arbor Paperbacks, 1961), p. 28.

been eloquently expressed by the behavior of the Captain hobbling along on an injured foot and of the Colonel striding first at the head of the column and later toward the rear.

The violence of the military institution even in peace is Styron's most damaging charge. In the opening sentences the death of eight Marines struck by misfired mortar shells points to the aimless waste of life, its reduction to a dead quantity: "It was not so much as if they had departed this life but as if, sprayed from a hose, they were only shreds of bone, gut, and dangling tissue to which it would have been impossible ever to impute the quality of life, far less the capacity to relinquish it."[3] Violence is the content of the days spent chasing a mock enemy. It is Mannix's way at last of preventing his company from giving up during the march when he fights the men who want to ride back to camp in trucks. And it marks the final authority behind the Colonel, who reaches for his revolver when Mannix opposes him. In the confusion, disorder, and displacement which the recall to military service brings, violence is the fundamental condition of what seems to Culver the "never-endingness of war" in the mid-twentieth century.

Being geared to violence, the military man cultivates qualities which the civilian considers worthless. Civilian life provided Culver and Mannix the alternation of daily work and relaxation with their families; military life offers them the simulated dangers of the training course and the sham pleasures of the garish officers' club. The military system makes strength falsely brutal by destroying compassion and tenderness. Living within the institution dehumanizes men to such an extent that the Colonel's inspection of Mannix's injured foot seems indecent, for "he had too long been conditioned by the system to perform with grace a human act."[4] Templeton is not wilfully cruel or vicious; he simply reduces all human beings to integers in the system.

But the very fact that the institution which depersonalizes

3. *The Long March* (New York: Random House, Modern Library Paperback, 1952), p. 3.
4. *Ibid.*, p. 89.

human relationships is itself impersonal makes revolt impossible.[5] This frustration is the germ of tragedy when men break themselves against the implacable for the sake of declaring their individuality in a judgment of right and wrong which the system will never recognize. Traditionally such rebellion has been treated with pity and respect as in a tragedy like *Antigone,* but in the twentieth century loss of belief in the power of the individual makes the protesting person an anachronism. Violence which might once have had meaning as the attempt of man to justify himself is now an absurd expenditure of energy and nerve. Instead of developing these tragic implications, however, Styron contents himself with statements of the case. Mannix is aware that his gestures are hopeless because they are individual rather than symbolic. The private rebellion, Styron says, merely mutilates the rebel. To make a genuine rebellion Mannix needed to be strong enough to care nothing for the false pride of completing the march, for in finishing the hike he and Culver accepted the values of the system they wished to defeat. The fundamental defeat is the fact that the institution has so shaped Mannix and Culver that they cannot effectively will to escape from it. "Another war," the author comments, "and years beyond reckoning, had violated their minds irrevocably."[6]

If such vitiation of the will has already occurred before the time of the novel, then the violence and the anguish of the rebellion seem nothing more than the imagined reflex of an amputated limb. In the end, Styron fails to make clear the meaning of the violence which Mannix represents. It may be the declaration of an individual who affirms himself by defying the institution, or it may be the death cry of an individual as he succumbs to the institution. A strong ironic commentary on the problem would result from a combination of the two

5. This power of military officialdom touched *The Long March* itself. In dramatizing the novel for television Styron was required to alter the theme and present a positive endorsement of military authority. See Styron's letter, "If You Write for Television . . . ," *The New Republic,* CXL (April 16, 1959), 16.
6. *Ibid.,* p. 69.

views, but the characterization and action in the novel are not adequately developed to make this statement. It is clear that Styron fears the inhumanity of institutionalized military life, and he has added another illustration to the bill of particulars which young writers have prepared since World War II, but he has not probed deeply into the problems of motivation and reaction. As a result, the violence of the emotions and the incidents in the novel seem present by external assignment rather than by inner necessity.

Because William Faulkner in particular among Southern writers has made the family an image of regional culture and history, it was inevitable that *Lie Down in Darkness* which chronicled the violent disintegration of a Southern family should be called Faulknerian. Similarities in subject and language were noted. In his candid use of violence Styron is akin to Faulkner, and like Faulkner, he composes elaborate rhythmical sentences meditating on human tragedy. But the similarities are merely faint echoes. The tone which Styron sustains is an elegiac hunger for integrity, firmness, conscience, and beauty. He does not sing of a golden past nor does he prophesy doom out of evil inherent in the past. What the code of the ancestors had to pass on was a sense of duty, kindness, and decency, but no one cared to listen. The Loftises of Port Warwick, Virginia, have chosen license rather than freedom, and like Ellen Glasgow's characters in *The Sheltered Life* they learn the littleness of their ventures. The web of personal failures which they know becomes a symbol of the tangled changes which threaten an entire society. In the novel the defeat is realized in the sordid relationships of persons who intended to approximate the leisure and ease of planter aristocracy. Their failure to appropriate any of the moral strength of a once orderly society precipitates the psychological illnesses which Styron describes.

Milton Loftis is an alcoholic enamored of his daughter Peyton; his wife Helen hates men and is pathologically jealous of Peyton; Maudie, the older daughter mentally and physically crippled from birth, dies of miliary tuberculosis; and Peyton, betrayed by both parents, commits suicide. The violent emotions and the guilt and shame of the family suggest the kind of collapse of discredited persons and times which occurs in Faulkner. In commenting on the tortured characters of the novel, John W. Aldridge, however, unnecessarily enlarges the elements of Southern melodrama which are latent in the breakup of the family. In his view the causes of disintegration are atavistic:

Behind Milton's father-guilt and incest guilt is the whole Southern blood-guilt. Behind Helen's jealousy and Puritanism is the timeless Southern gentlewoman madness, the madness that comes from too much inbreeding, too much Negro fear, too much sexual neglect. Behind Peyton's father-complex is a century of paternalism and man-hatred and sexual masochism.[7]

The error in this formidable array of motivation is that Styron's view of the Southern past is considerably more charitable than this statement suggests. Milton in remembering his father, for example, recalls not only that the old man gave fatuous advice and failed to discipline his son adequately but also that he understood the weakness of his son and the strain to which a non-heroic world would subject him. In *Set This House on Fire*, Styron indicates even more explicitly that the Southern past contained ideals worth conserving. The narrator Peter Leverett admires the liberalism of his old father, who feels that "we've sold our birthright, and old Tom Jefferson is spinning in his grave."[8] The fatal erosion of Milton's character it seems must be attributed as much to the unfortunate effects of social changes in the present as to radical psychological defects in the Southern past.

In their dedication to pleasure, the Loftises substitute self-indulgence for duty, a shift in mores which Ellen Glasgow also charted. The violence which this new allegiance introduces is more frankly portrayed by Styron than by Miss Glas-

7. *In Search of Heresy: American Literature in an Age of Conformity* (New York: McGraw-Hill Book Company, Inc., 1956), pp. 146-147.
8. *Set This House on Fire* (New York: Random House, 1960), p. 15.

gow, but a similar corruption of the strength and loyalty which Southern families once represented appears in the fiction of both writers. Helen Loftis remembers that "she had wanted the future to be like a nice, long, congenial tea party, where everyone talked a little, danced a little and had polite manners."[9] She is an extension of the new young woman whom Miss Glasgow observed defying traditional social standards in order to please herself, a sister to characters like Jenny Blair, Roy Timberlake, and Annabel Upchurch. When Roy, Asa Timberlake's divorced daughter in *In This Our Life*, hears her father talk about the responsibility and integrity required to maintain a marriage, she dismisses his ideas as meaningless words to be replaced by the fact of her private happiness. Mrs. Upchurch in *The Romantic Comedians*, hurt by her daughter's headstrong selfishness, pursues her duty with the feeling "that there were no longer any moral properties left in the world. Experience was reduced to the sum of pure egoism."[10] In Styron's novels the result of such egocentrism always is violent destruction.

Neither Helen nor Milton Loftis wants to be an adult, morally or emotionally. Made financially independent by Helen's inheritance, they build an expensive home and join the country club set. In this life Styron shows the middle class abandoning its Puritan principles of vocation and thrift, its moral code and respectability, and affecting the mannerisms of the wealthy and the leisured. Without a social structure of values to support them, the Loftises have no interior strength to curb their weaknesses. In a Southern community these disabilities stand out clearly because there is the memory of another standard by which to gauge the violence of change.

The personal violence which eventually shatters the marriage of Helen and Milton appears first in Helen's pathological possessiveness. Her breakdown is the one most elaborately de-

9. *Lie Down in Darkness* (Indianapolis: The Bobbs-Merrill Company, Inc., 1951), p. 273.
10. *The Romantic Comedians* (New York: Doubleday, Page and Company, 1926), p. 300.

tailed in the novel and serves as the focus of violence for the entire family. The crushing accumulation of violence is supported structurally by the circuitous chronology of the novel as the action moves back and forth between the immediate present when Milton and Dolly, Helen having refused, have driven to the railway station to meet Peyton's coffin and the past which has led to this end. In each chapter an incident of Helen's irrationality appears. These steadily build tension, from Helen's accusations that Milton dislikes Maudie and that Peyton tried to injure the girl, through her outbursts which ruin parties, to the fight between mother and daughter at Peyton's wedding. Helen converts the festivities of an ordinary middleclass family into sordid incidents of anger, jealousy, and hatred. These violent emotions at first seem the symptoms of neuroticism, but as the novel progresses, passages from Helen's subconsciousness reveal that she is insane. In dreams she wanders through a landscape where decomposing corpses of females, especially Milton's mistress Dolly and —Helen eventually admits to herself—Peyton, lie broken to her power. At the wedding reception her ravings to the rector Carey Carr cause him to exclaim, "You are mad."[11] And Dr. Holcomb watches stupefied as Helen looks around the room for Peyton: "With her arms at her side stiff as sticks, only her head moved and her blue, crazy eyes: it was like watching an adder, thought the doctor; surely she was ready to strike."[12]

Styron can make the violence of Helen believable and important partly because insanity has its own fascination, but he must work even more skilfully with Milton. That the disintegration of this weak, self-indulgent person matters is the triumph of tone. Styron is neither clinically objective nor abusively ironic. He is compassionate toward Milton but never toward Milton's waste of himself and others. Loftis merely dabbles at his law practice, and his conviviality quickly degenerates into alcoholism. He wants Peyton to be the adult in

11. *Lie Down in Darkness*, p. 300.
12. *Ibid.*, p. 305.

his life, a demand she unequivocally refuses when he confesses to her his infantile behavior during the day that he left Helen with the dying Maudie and joined the football game festivities, ending finally by getting drunk and falling into a culvert. Awash in self-pity, he is not once capable of the discipline which Peyton rightfully wants, which might curb Helen, and which would save himself. Added to his natural weakness is the pressure of a social environment which from his college days onward has instructed him to insist first on his personal gratifications.

Peyton, like Caddy Compson in *The Sound and the Fury*, is the victim of the failure of her parents and of her society. She has never defied convention so wildly as Helen claims, and her summary of the rebellion of her generation is simple: ". . . most kids these days are not wrong or wrongdoers, they're just aimless and lost, more aimless than you all ever thought of being. . . ."[13] All they really want is to come home and to give love as a welcome duty owed to parents who have cared for them. She hates the pretense of the blissful family which Helen wants to maintain. Just before her wedding she exclaims to her father, "Oh, I feel so sorry for us all. If just she'd had a soul and you'd had some guts. . . ."[14] Later to Helen she enumerates her mother's neurotic reactions and asserts her own right to be free and to work to become happy. The clarity of Peyton's analysis, however, cannot save her from disaster. Styron, assuming that the motivation of her collapse is implicit in the history of her family, details her breakdown only for the day of her suicide. The stream-of-consciousness passage in which he follows her until she jumps from a twelfth-floor window is a flow of memories, guilt feelings, and nameless terrors. Instead of the quarreling and infidelity of her life, she longs for the cessation of violence. She dreams of a clock, perfect and perpetual, in which she would "sleep forever, yet not really sleep, but remain only half-aware of time and enclosed

13. *Ibid.*, p. 268.
14. *Ibid.*, pp. 268-269.

by it as in a womb of brass, revolving on that spring like a dead horse on a merry-go-round."[15] Caddy as victim is sinister, deliberately seeking evil; Peyton is pitiable, wanting another choice but being incapable of making it.

Because Styron never expresses the violence between Helen and Milton in physical action until their final encounter at Peyton's funeral, the melodramatic frenzy of Milton at this time is genuinely climactic, and Styron's rhetorical flight carries the passion. Outside the chapel where Peyton's body lies, Milton makes a last appeal to Helen and then tries to choke her when she rebuffs him. Transfixed by the violence he has witnessed, Cary Carr imagines a ghostly sound stirring from within the chapel which echoes the ruin he has been powerless to prevent.

Paralleling the collapse of the family in this novel is the failure of religion. Helen had dismissed religion as a toy although she liked to use it to dramatize her paranoia. Carey Carr as the official representative of the church, tries to share the violence of the Loftis family and to deepen his own religious experience, but he has no extraordinary vision. Only the Negroes of the novel have the capacity to love and to believe. Like Faulkner's Dilsey, Ella Swan, the Loftises' maid, has religious faith, and perhaps like Dilsey will therefore endure. The novel closes with a carnival of religion. Ella Swan joins Daddy Faith's adherents by the waterside for a noisy evening service rich in panoply and hypnotic ritual. In the midst of the garish symbols that decorate the pulpit on a raft and the vestments of his attendants, Daddy Faith appears as plain and genuine as the truth which Carr had yearned to make real to Helen and Milton. The world of the Loftises has gone to pieces violently, but Daddy Faith promises, "De grass withereth, de flower fadeth, but de world of your God shall stand forever."[16]

The moral decay which destroys the Loftises becomes the

15. *Ibid.*, p. 335.
16. *Ibid.*, p. 399.

subject of violence in *Set This House on Fire*. Isolated in
Italy, Styron's Americans act out the moral and spiritual an-
archy which the author believes threatens to ruin their nation.
The interplay between the North represented by Mason
Flagg, the profligate playboy, and the South represented by
Peter Leverett, the narrator who is alternately fascinated and
repelled by the sordid lives of Flagg and his coterie, suggests
that Styron's criticism of American culture is in part praise
for the South's resistance to materialism. But it is also a warning against assuming that the South is free from error, for,
writing of his schoolboy friendship with Mason, Peter remarks,
"In the end I was the only friend he had left—which as I look
at it now may well have been a measure of my corruptibil-
ity."[17] The lure of Mason's wealth, sophistication, and affected
ennui introduced into the middle-class, conservative Virginia
society which nurtured Peter continues to operate until the
violence of Flagg's adult life shocks Peter into recognizing
its apparent brilliance and freedom for futility and perversion. The sense of judgment which Flagg's morbid domination
of the artist Cass Kinsolving finally awakens in Leverett is
rooted in the moral values of the society in which Peter grew
up. In the opening pages of the novel Styron depicts the hon-
esty of Peter's father, his devotion to duty and justice, and his
love for the beauty of the South, now passing into shopping
centers and parking lots. These are the touchstones for meas-
uring the degradation of Mason and America.

Through his money and subtly exerted homosexual attraction, Mason has enormous power, especially over someone
as improvident and neurotic as Cass, but Styron holds Cass
responsible for his own condition. His drunkenness, his crippling lack of confidence in his ability to paint, his dreary self-
pity, and finally his murder of Flagg come from a lack of faith.
During the week end when Cass and Peter thrash out the
meaning of the violence they had endured in Italy, Cass
admits the lack of freedom in the aimlessness of his life in

17. *Set This House on Fire*, p. 75.

Europe when he was trapped, as he says, by terror, booze, and self. Throughout the long probing by Peter to fathom the real relationship between Cass and Mason, Cass reiterates that he was to blame for the misery of his life. Killing Mason because presumably he had raped the beautiful peasant girl Francesca was in truth a rationalization for an act of violence to exorcise the evil in his own being. The fact that as an orphan he had felt abandoned and that the United States had seemed to him a "smart-Alex, soft-headed, baby-faced, pre-digested, cellophane wrapped, doomed, beauty-hating, land" could not extenuate his guilt.[18] "I suspect," he had written in his journal, "that whosoever it is that rises in a dream with a look on his face of eternal damnation is just ones own self, wearing a mask, and that's the fact of the matter."[19]

Like one of Flannery O'Connor's characters, Cass by violence arrives at the knowledge that his loneliness and his demonic impulses are symptoms of his estrangement from faith which would free him from despair, hatred, and terror. His willingness to let Mason humiliate him in exchange for food and liquor paradoxically becomes the means of his deliverance to decent human freedom. Through Mason he secures drugs to treat Francesca's tubercular father and thus by converting his dependence into a voluntary act to save another, he frees himself from the control of Mason. This spiritual change, however, is not evident to him until long after the hours of horror during which Francesca is raped and fatally mutilated by the village idiot, and Cass murders Mason. Having denied his talent because he was afraid to risk the discipline it required and having destroyed another man by the bestiality in himself, Cass has dropped as far into the existential abyss of nothingness as any other character in recent fiction. Captain Mannix has an ever-present symbol of the cause of his misery in Colonel Templeton, the embodiment of the military juggernaut; Milton Loftis only dimly compre-

18. *Ibid.*, p. 364.
19. *Ibid.*

hends the enormity of his blunders; but Cass Kinsolving is fully conscious that he alone elected the fatal course he was following until by an act of will he turns its violence into a force for life rather than death. Cass begins to return from despair by an affirmation of being. He achieves no faith to approximate that of his Catholic wife or that of the Negroes or even of Carey Carr, but violence brings him to understand

that as for being and nothingness, the one thing I did know was that to choose between them was simply to choose being, not for the sake of being, or even the love of being, much less the desire to be forever—but in the hope of being what I could be for a time. This would be an ecstasy. God knows, it would.[20]

Formal institutional expressions of morality have no urgency for Cass whatsoever, but he finds that his denial of a moral dimension provokes death and destruction. When Cass "comes back," it is to the South where both he and Peter begin to rediscover the spiritual strength which their drifting in the wake of Mason's wealth and libertinism had vitiated.

Victimized by an institution like the military organization and failed by institutions like the family and the church, Styron's characters move toward ruin. The violence which they initiate or endure marks either the clash of the individual with an organization impervious to his needs or his struggle to live in the vacuum left by the dispersion of social and moral patterns. In both instances his efforts are complicated by his own private failure of resolution. The defeated men in *The Long March* are types of the modern non-hero, who, as William Barrett observes, "is at once everyman and nobody."[21] In *Lie Down in Darkness* Styron makes the helplessly weak person matter, not by arousing bathetic sentiment for him but by projecting his failure as a sign of human vulnerability. In the foreground is the frailty of man's will and in the background is the fall of a society which denies its ideals. Styron moves on in *Set This House on Fire* to demand that the weak

20. *Ibid.*, pp. 500-501.
21. *Irrational Man: A Study in Existential Philosophy* (Garden City: Doubleday and Company, Inc., 1958), p. 54.

person accept his own culpability for this fall by having chosen to destroy when he might create. In each crisis violence signals the moral disruption and is the suffering through which freedom may come.

V. The voices of distance: William Goyen

William Goyen, like Robert Penn Warren, may be called a border Southerner, because he was born at Trinity, Texas, in 1915, and grew up in Houston. Along this eastern edge of the state the settlers and their farm economy were extensions of the older Southern states. These people are Southern rather than Southwestern in such points as their attitudes toward family and Negroes, in the tempo of their life, and in their speech. The humid, somnolent pine woods and cotton fields are not unlike Georgia. It is this country and its people that Goyen recalls in most of his fiction. He differs markedly from his contemporaries in his lyrical, poetic translation of material into his imagined world. Mood finally supplants place. When the specifications of place and people fade, the violence becomes grotesqueness. The shadowy, elusive figures drop the forthrightness of violence and take on the half-lights, the mysteries, and the freakishness of the grotesque. Although their existence often seems other-worldly, these ghosts are related to the fear of crass industrialism and standardization which haunts or has haunted many Southerners.

Goyen has published five books: *The House of Breath* (1950), *Ghost and Flesh* (1952), *In a Farther Country* (1955), *The Faces of Blood Kindred* (1960), and *The Fair Sister* (1963). Each is a collection of short pieces related in theme and mood. The most recent book is the briefest and the most unified, having been developed from a single story. Currently Goyen lives in New York, where he teaches a course in the modern novel and directs a playwright's workshop at the New School.

Foremost in Goyen's work is a sense that human life now has no integrity. People are isolated from one another and from the past. They have lost their purpose, their ideals, and their capacity to communicate with one another. These psychological and moral disorders parallel the intrusion of industry, which has obliterated natural beauty and set profit above love and community. The grotesqueness of spiritual injuries and of physical malformations which manifests these conditions as well as overt violence interests Goyen. He creates an atmosphere of horror and ugliness in which characters are suspended like figures in a half-forgotten nightmare. In this environment ghosts thrive, or living people take on ghosthood before actual death, as if they were too passive either to live or to die. The effect depends less on the trappings of Southern Gothic in the sense of decayed landscapes, corrupted families, and sudden violence than upon the distortion in the character's mind and spirit. The mood is one of negation: man is lost, alone, bewildered, and disinherited. There is little evidence that he can be restored although he searches for aspirations to lift him and for others with whom to share himself. Heroism has been reduced to a grim suffering of unhappiness. The possibility of beginning again is the only relief, and without it "the rest is death: murder (self or other), betrayal, violence and cruelty, vengeance and crimes of fear."[1]

The subtlety with which Goyen perceives introspective characters and expresses their reveries approaches a kind of literary neuroticism. The dominant mood both of the characters and narrators is self-pity; hence there is little analysis of motives and causation. Action, conflict, and change as elements of drama in fiction are less important than the medita-

---

1. "The Horse and the Day Moth," *The Faces of Blood Kindred: A Novella and Ten Stories* (New York: Random House, 1960), p. 158.

tions of the narrator upon them. In this temper Goyen conveys something of the emotional stagnation and isolation of modern man as seen by Albert Camus in *L'Etranger* and Jean-Paul Sartre in *La Nausée*. Goyen's characters, however, do not engage in philosophical quests to define existence, for they are solaced simply by reciting their laments.

It may be that Goyen and other Southerners are peculiarly sensitive to the distance between them and their fellows because they grew up in a region where the knowledge that it had lost a war and wealth to the North was a part of the spiritual matrix of its people. Furthermore, since the thirties, Southerners have been newly aware that the more nearly they become standardized workers and consumers, the more radically they alter the mores of their regional culture. In Goyen's fiction the feeling of being isolated is not so much expressed in dramatic situations as it makes up the circumambient mood in which life looks broken like a stick refracted in water. A view of this brokenness is made possible by the emotional distance between the narrator and the people he writes about. Because the narrator's role is to convince the reader to accept the vision of distortion, the method of narration is especially important.

To make vivid the malady of isolation and the consequent violent disintegration of human relationships, Goyen relies upon a point of view which might be called multiple refraction. This method is best exemplified in *The House of Breath* in which the narrator is a young man who speaks for himself both in the present and in the past, a period he captures by reconstructing the biographies of members of his family. The one quality he is able to respond to in each person is isolation. The fact that these people are warped further disjoints the narrative line. Before the grotesque personalities reach the reader, their characterization has been filtered through their own consciousnesses and through two time levels in the narrator's mind. Wrapped thus in several layers of subjective responses, the people tend never to come alive. Under this treatment violence is chiefly a matter of tensions which are repressed and action which occurs only in report. In the novel *In a Farther Country* the relation between the reader and the event is less distant because part of the narrative is conveyed dramatically, but the dream device which forms a large portion of the book forces the reader's attention to follow a refraction again from Marietta's actual life into her fantasies and on to the narrator's commentary. The method of narration varies in *Ghost and Flesh;* a story like "The White Rooster" is almost entirely dramatic, but "Pore Perrie" is reflected from the narrator and from Aunt Linsie. No other writer in the groups studied here makes use of such refraction to enhance the distance from the norm which grotesque characters already represent. The effect is to heighten the sense of isolation in Goyen's work and simultaneously to reduce its dramatic impact. Because the themes which the violent and grotesque underscore are presented obliquely and at several removes from everyday actuality, Goyen seems to construct his fictional world from an entirely private view, whereas an author like Eudora Welty, who uses similar themes, moves toward the collective human experience in myth and legend.

Evidence of the breaking apart of the world in Goyen's work appears in the disintegration of family and town, the absence of beauty and the presence of the disfigured, the lack of communication between human beings, the conflict of generations, and the meaninglessness of human endeavor. The inadequacies of the family are delineated in the disordered and eroded lives of the Ganchions which the narrator recalls in *The House of Breath*. Three generations occupied the house during the time that Boy, the speaker, lived there, but they failed one another. Their isolation is emphasized by the epigraphs on the title page; Aunt Malley's question, "What kin are we all to each other, anyway?" and Rimbaud's declaration, *"Je est un autre."* Goyen is hurt by the separateness which he sees. In contrast, Eudora Welty cherishes the essen-

tial privacy of the Fairchilds in *Delta Wedding* as an ineluc-
table mystery which enhances their humanity.

The sign of man's separation from himself and from others
is the ghost. It is also the mark of the lost parts of life which
have become invisible but demand union with the visible in
order to restore wholeness. The widow of Raymon Emmons,
for example, has driven her husband to suicide by her coldness and pretensions to superiority, but her guilt achieves a
strange resurrection of the man she despised in life. She reports with wonder, "Comes ridin onto the sleepinporch ever
night regular as clockwork, ties iz horse to the bedstead and
I say hello Raymon Emmons and we start our conversation."[2] Through Mrs. Emmons' Ancient Mariner compulsion
to tell that she learned to welcome the ghost of the husband
by loving and losing another man, Goyen makes explicit the
rhythm of alternation which he considers the basic pattern of
life: "And I think that ghosts, if you set still with em long
enough, can give you over to flesh 'n bones; and that flesh 'n
bones, if you go roun when it's time, can send you back to
a faithful ghost. One provides the other."[3] To make life something valuable is not a matter of renouncing the material for
the sake of the spiritual but of recognizing that they occupy
different but complementary worlds.

The three women in "The Letter in the Cedarchest" who
traffic with ghosts want nothing more than a household "that
will let us be the way we are."[4] Since church and marriage
have failed them, they have only their own eccentricities to
cultivate. By humoring Little Pigeon's insanity, Lucille and
Sammye live in a cloud cuckoo land, but they preserve the
virtues of generosity, patience, courtesy, and kindness. By
letting it be the deranged who perceive the possibility of
order and meaning in a disordered world, Goyen makes the

2. "Ghost and Flesh, Water and Dirt," *Ghost and Flesh* (New York:
Random House, 1952), p. 87.
3. *Ibid.*, p. 89.
4. *Ibid.*, p. 51.

old truths of love and integrity stand out with new sharpness.

Violence in Goyen's fiction is most likely to erupt when past and present collide, as happens in Miss O'Connor's stories also. The hatred and misunderstanding which arise from the conflict of generations notably dominate one story, "The White Rooster." The battered but confident white rooster which defies Marcy Samuels is easily identified with her irritating father-in-law, and the trap which her husband builds to catch the fowl seems to Grandpa the first step in his own destruction. On the afternoon when the rooster steps to the edge of the trap and Marcy watches eagerly to drop the door, Grandpa glides his wheel chair behind Marcy and strikes her down with his hunting knife. He then rolls through the house in a tornado of destruction. The description of his savagery is a vigorous report:

... he threw up pots and pans in the kitchen, was in the flour and sugar like a whirlwind, overturned chairs and ripped the upholstery in the living room until the stuffing flew in the air; and covered with straw and flour, white like a demented ghost, he flayed the bedroom wallpaper into hanging shreds; coughing and howling, he lashed and wrecked and razed until he thought he was bringing the very house down upon himself.[5]

The orgy of violence, as irrational as the hatred between Grandpa and Marcy, is a startling comment on the fury of age. It is as if the past, feeling itself threatened, turned in an insane rage to demolish the present. No reconciliation after violence is possible here as it is in Robert Penn Warren's novels.

Criticism of modern life as being impersonal, mechanical, and ruthless is implicit throughout Goyen's work. Hostility to industrialism is expressed by the unhappy lives of characters passed in dreary surroundings. The maladjustments caused by the change from a farm economy to an industrial economy alarm him less than the destruction of natural beauty and social graciousness. His indictment of industry, urbanization, and greed for profits never precipitates the kind of violence

5. *Ibid.*, p. 22.

which sets farmer against farmer in *Night Rider* or demolishes humaneness in *Tobacco Road*. Instead, Goyen portrays an attrition of life whereby a family like the Ganchions in *The House of Breath* decays and disintegrates, withdrawing into blindness, insanity, and perversion, or a sensitive person like Marietta McGee-Chavéz retires into her fantasies of the good life "in a farther country."

The background for the Ganchions is a rural Texas town Charity, a counterpart to Goyen's birthplace, where a sawmill and oil wells have disfigured the countryside and corrupted the people. These industries pollute both men and nature. The fertile bottomlands and the once fresh river now reek with slime. People deceive and cheat for the sake of money and thus obliterate their real identities. Even the name of the town has become a lie. Misery and potential violence roil under the surface of a town where once the good order of agrarianism promised beauty and satisfaction. Aunt Malley muses that "the world has sold away everything that was beautiful and as the Lord put it here to be, human beins have changed everything into money and show."[6]

The town has given birth to freaks—babies with swollen heads and bloated bodies, deaf mutes, and a "frogboy"—products, as it were, of moral as well as physical decay. The Ganchions who tried to escape to find loveliness failed as miserably as those who stayed to rot. Sue Emma sold her love and beauty. Folner ran away with a show because it promised glitter and brilliance, but he deviated into homosexuality and soon committed suicide. The narrator, remembering the disgust which Folner felt for the dismal incompleteness of life in Charity comments:

> You were tinsel all the way, beautiful boy Folner, all the rotten way. Once I said, building a chicken coop, 'I want to make this *right*.'
> 'Nothing is made right around here, Boy,' you said. 'Everything is crooked and warped and twisted.'[7]

6. *The House of Breath* (New York: Random House, 1950), p. 78.
7. *Ibid.*, p. 114.

Normal human relations, Goyen emphasizes, are impossible where profit supplants beauty, and integrity collapses.

Christy, another of Granny Ganchion's sons, had waited for Otey Bell, his wife, to grow up and permit him to touch her. In *Tobacco Road* this kind of situation is grotesquely full of life because Lov has an eye for other women and there is the implication that Pearl will eventually find sexual adventures in the city if not at home; Goyen, however, converts the symbolic sexual death to an unnatural fulfilment in death. Otey Bell drowns, and in drawing her lifeless, naked body up through the water Christy feels that for the first time she has surrendered to him. Instead of experiencing a rebirth from the water into life, Christy is satisfied with death.

Despite the blame which Goyen attaches to industrialism for destroying spirit and beauty, the death and defeat which come to the Ganchions largely reflect the melancholia of the narrator. He describes the meaninglessness of life which he believes most people conspire to conceal even from themselves. In concentrating on his personal response to the distasteful circumstances of life, Goyen cultivates romantic gloom rather than a sense of life as essentially tragic. Tenderness and regret for lost ways of living replace pity for the inexorable demands of life and man's inability to answer them. The grotesqueness and freakishness of human behavior and appearance in his work is a product of the author's emotional set, not of a social theory as in Caldwell or of a view of destiny as in Faulkner.

In order to replace the ugliness of the external world with love and beauty, Goyen creates a fantasy world where people can communicate, but only on the terms imagined by the author of the new world. Marietta McGee-Chavéz is Goyen's agent for restoring the maimed and fragmented to wholeness in the novel *In a Farther Country*. The need to convert the intolerable everyday experience of a chaotic world into desirable order leads Goyen into dream and fantasy. Marietta working in a shop in New York is cut off from the natural beauty and the inspiration to create which she knew in her hidden valley in New Mexico, for as she says, ". . . the dream of the whole seems accomplished only in the work of nature and eternally fails in human nature's artifice."[8] In New York hopes are buried under noise, hasty crowds, and neon signs which announce the instability of human relations in the words "Moving and Storage." One specially decorated room in her apartment she calls Spain, the haven of beauty and truth, where in her dreams she receives a group of the dispossessed —murderers, disappointed lovers, a poetess, a nun and a priest, and a would-be suicide. To these voices telling their grotesque or violent stories she listens with the sympathy and acceptance of an impartial mother. This action is sufficient to restore the lost pattern to each of the lives and to fulfill the ideal voiced by the young man in "Nests in a Stone Image": "to bring love into all the dark lonely rooms. . . ."[9]

Goyen views the lack of community in the modern world fundamentally as a failure of communication. Although in *The Faces of Blood Kindred, The House of Breath,* and *In a Farther Country* he considers factories and cities obstacles to communication between human beings, he indicates that the state of mind which denies the past isolates people even more dangerously and thrusts them into eccentricity or violence. Because it is never clear what form a positive relationship with the past would take, most of the characters remain caught in confusion and disorder as if these conditions were nets which tightened in direct proportion to the pressure of the struggle against them. The past which the narrators in Goyen's fiction wish to restate in terms of a unified present has little relation to the historical past of the South. Instead they work from private memories of grotesqueness, violence, and ugliness which they have noted in the lives around them. Their sense that it is evil to cut off the past is, however, a peculiarly Southern heritage. They seek to reunite warring elements within a

8. *In a Farther Country* (New York: Random House, 1955), p. 12.
9. *Ghost and Flesh*, p. 145.

single personality or to relate the person to history and society in ways which will calm the violence without damaging the freedom of the individual.

Goyen's most elusive evocation of the past and the loss of community is Old Somebody, a Wandering Jew figure who from birth was brought up in the woods like a forest animal. In old age as he wanders from house to house he is a reminder of the past, of "Our Old Ancestry," which perpetuates itself from person to person, and of our mortality which succumbs to the dust. Children listen to him to learn how to communicate with the past in order to make confusion and violence significant. Their parents cannot teach them because in a present devoted to buying and selling, all the moral, aesthetic, and passionate sources of life are dry. What was once community is now broken into mere real estate, and the inhabitants are set against one another. As a result, the speaker mourns, ". . . our feet have been broken by the ways we have gone, . . . and the blood of our feet stains the wave and the dust."[10] A similar character is Boney Benson, by day a railroadman, by night a ghostly rider pursuing a shape of light. The ineffable quality of communication is symbolized for the teller of the tale in his memory of Benson's having once taken his kite and run a message up the string until the kite and message broke away and sailed off where words do not exist.

Left wordless in the ordinary world, characters turn violent. The most extreme behavior develops when a character can communicate with neither the past nor the present. Jack Flanders, for example, lost his tie with the past when his father deserted the family and was found years later freed from a penitentiary but paralyzed and speechless. The young man's desire to be an actor was frustrated because his heritage was nothing but "mysterious crime and speechlessness."[11] In despair he tried to commit suicide by slashing his face. The pain of trying to destroy himself subsides only when he re-

10. "Children of Old Somebody," *Ghost and Flesh*, p. 128.
11. *In a Farther Country*, p. 134.

moves the beard which hides his scars and speaks to the
listeners in Marietta's apartment. The artist's problem of communication has an obvious interest for Goyen, whose artist
characters find that the rift between past and present produces violence or stimulates the grotesque in their imagination. Then discordant elements can be reconciled only in the
act of communication when the other exists as a receiver who
makes the struggle to achieve integrity worthwhile.

Although Goyen abhors the loss of the past and the growth
of cities as signs of the wrong direction which modern civilization has taken, he also sees that rigid resistance to change
carries its own dangers. Princis Lester takes her Red River
Country ways with her to Houston when she marries. Her
story in *The Faces of Blood Kindred* relates that the city
neighbors rather admire her sunbonnets and her refusal to
shop in a supermarket, but quaintness will not save Princis.
The final result of her inflexibility is insanity. In choosing to
withdraw and shut herself away from others, she degenerates
into a bewildered animal. Finally, like her sisters, she grows
a beard, the mark of their eccentric inheritance.

In other explorations of time Goyen treats the passage from
past to future as a change in personality. Often the initiation
of children into the meaning of time requires violence and disorder. Boy in *The House of Breath* experiences a symbolic
destruction of his old self and the birth of a new being when
Christy leads him into a thicket on a hunting trip. Goyen portrays the change by images of violence, a method of finding
parallel metaphors for disturbed psyches. Thus Goyen first
pictures the reflection of the boy in a pool and then shatters it
when Christy shoots a snake gliding across the surface. Later
by flinging away the necklace of birds killed by Christy which
he has been wearing, the boy discards his own dead past.
These acts finally free him from his potentially dangerous association with Christy. The adolescent girl Quella, from whose
point of view "The Grasshopper's Burden" is told, perceives
that the passing of time is the coming of death. In this story

George Kurunus, a child painfully handicapped by cerebral palsy, is an image of disorder and imperfection. Deformed and repulsive in appearance, George stumbles along at the end of a straight line of marching students, "the capricious conclusion and mocking collapse of something all ordered and precise right up to the tag end."[12] His grasshopper-like face at a window prefigures the ravage of time, "an appetite or a desire that would surely, one day, get them every one; all the beautiful schoolchildren gathered and moving like the chosen through the heavenly amber afternoon light. . . ."[13] His ugly grotesqueness is a form of death in life, an emblem like the skeletons which dance with living human beings in medieval pictures of the *danse macabre*. In "Old Wildwood" a grandfather with a deformed foot is the bridge between his grandson's past and future. Through the old man's celebration of the violence and energy of their pioneer forebears, the boy comes to realize that his grandfather's drinking and women, his ruthless independence, and even his misshapen foot express a vigor which he wants to memorialize in a world of flat, insipid lives.

Goyen's experiments with themes and narrators culminate in the voice of Ruby Drew in *The Fair Sister*. The words and rhythms of this voice encompass only so much violence and grotesquerie as are needed to complete the myth in which the claims of flesh and soul, mind and heart, words and acts cross one another like threads in a tapestry. The fair sister Savata and the dark sister Ruby Drew, who are Negro Jews, unite in themselves the hopes and losses of two minorities. Strong in soul and words, Ruby Drew struggles to draw the voluptuous Savata from a night club into a church under the instruction of the dazzling Prince o' Light, who takes exercises to induce continence. The two sisters convert a store in Brooklyn into the Light of the World Holiness Church, where Savata stars as bishop. A raucous congregation of human oddments re-

12. *Ghost and Flesh*, p. 101.
13. *Ibid.*, p. 110.

sponds to the magnetic Savata in an excess of spirit, but the spirit is falsified by Savata and the new business manager Canaan Johnson, facile with words and sleekly dressed in a black suit with red lapels, for their egocentric energies turn the Light of the World into money and bright lights on a marquee. The dark sister respects the vitality of Savata but fights the weaknesses which incapacitate the spirit. Savata's trafficking with press agents and Canaan Johnson's absconding with the church funds cannot diminish her faith, but Ruby Drew is left with a church from which the glamour as well as the violence has departed.

The battle in this tale is no longer between the self and an outside world ruined by machines and warehouses but between the body and the soul, neither sufficient by itself to make a complete human being. The frenzy which in Goyen's earlier books broke into violence is now channeled toward tolerance. The narrating voice speaks with assurance in its own rhythm and imagery; it retains the incantatory tone of preceding narrators but with increased authority and extended range. Sounds from Southern revival sermons echo in Ruby Drew's statements punctuated by "thank you Jesus." Ruby Drew can admit that "something got aholt of me and just possessed me, some demon that still lived in those clothes of glory out of Savata's show trunk," or she can persuade, "For I shall lead you to the pure river, where the sun shines on the waters and nothing but sunshine falls all day, and a garden of paradise, complete with fruits and flowering trees, invites you to walk in it, *without snakes*."[14] Whether confessing or pleading, defying or exhorting, she can look on the violence of lust and betrayal with "faith and human compassion."[15]

Because Goyen's fiction is introspective and descriptive of moods rather than objectively dramatic, it depends more upon grotesqueness than upon violence to portray the author's vision of a world askew. Although Goyen reacts to many of

14. *The Fair Sister* (New York: Doubleday and Company, 1963), pp. 27, 96.
15. *Ibid.*, p. 28.

the same flaws of man and society which arouse his fellow writers in the South, his method creates a nebulous haunting effect at the opposite pole from the naturalism of Erskine Caldwell. The studied remoteness of the narrators, their brooding over their observations, and the shading into fantasy and symbol shape the kind of prose which Goyen himself described when he said, "I think prose has the right to be lyrical, to sing. It has the right to be a miracle, to contain the miraculous."[16] His prose is finely wrought. Vowels are arranged for their melody. Rhythms—whether of folk speech or of standard written prose—are subtly adjusted to the tone and mood. The metaphors and symbols suggest the death, coldness, and isolation which permeate much of Goyen's world. Such technical adroitness sometimes calls excessive attention to itself, and the language becomes a trick obfuscation of simple materials. When this happens, Goyen's mourning for beauty and truth seems a private elegy too fragile for translation. When he succeeds in controlling and uniting both subject and style, as he does notably in *The Fair Sister*, he leads the reader along the uncertain line between the normal and the abnormal, the sane and the insane, the actual and the myth. The people and the landscapes from which fantasy is evoked are generally Southern, and the values that have been violated until the narrators are moved to despair are those which have particular significance in Southern culture: the unity of the family, personal integrity, a constructive relationship between past and present, and an economic order sensitive to human beings and natural beauty.

16. Harvey Breit, "Talk with William Goyen," *New York Times Book Review*, Sept. 10, 1950, p. 12.

VI. Violence in a private world: Truman Capote

The private quality of violence and grotesqueness in William Goyen's fiction is even more pronounced in the work of Truman Capote. Again the artist appears alone and isolated; custom and tradition scarcely impinge on his personal world enough to provoke him to rebel. Capote, however, creates characters who—at least for the time that the reader is in their world—have an intensity and reality more convincing than that of many of Goyen's people, muffled as the latter frequently are by the memory of the narrator. To a greater degree than Goyen, he constructs his fiction with specific data graphically presented. Thus the violent and the grotesque elements in it have a firm circumstantial existence.

Where Goyen sets up a mixed, often nightmarish, world unrelieved except by fancies like those of Marietta McGee-Chavéz and the faith of Ruby Drew, Capote creates two worlds: one contains the dark disorder of man's life and the other embodies the cheer of innocent love and beauty. The first, as Paul Levine has pointed out, is an "inverted nocturnal world," and the second is "realistic, colloquial, often humorous daytime."[1] In this first world, radical fear with its accompanying violence dominates; in the latter Capote's talent for humor and fanciful episodes has full play. Having made this kind of division, Capote is content to stay entirely within his created worlds, while Goyen through either his narrator's editorializing or, less often, the comment of a character conveys a sense of a larger world outside his creation to which his

1. "Truman Capote: The Revelation of the Broken Image," *Virginia Quarterly Review*, XXXIV (Fall, 1958), 602.

creation should be related. The Boy who returns to the Ganchion household, for example, comes from war service and vagabondage to look for understanding which will help him go back into the public world and live with meaning. A passage between the actual world and the imagined world, however, is scarcely hinted in Capote's work with the exception of *Other Voices, Other Rooms*, where Joel's losing touch with his previous ordinary life in New Orleans presages his perversion by the abnormal life at Skully's Landing. In general, therefore, the violence which Capote portrays has an immediate application confined largely to the boundaries of his imagination.

Capote's first novel, *Other Voices, Other Rooms*, which appeared in 1948 when the author was twenty-four years old, was widely discussed. Not only did his writing receive excited attention, but his personality became a minor literary legend. The following year he brought out a collection of short stories, *A Tree of Night and Other Stories*. Since then he has published two novels, *The Grass Harp* (1951) and *Breakfast at Tiffany's* (1958), three short stories appearing with the novella in the latter volume. In 1952 he successfully dramatized *The Grass Harp* for a Broadway production, and in 1954 his musical play, *House of Flowers*, was performed. His observations about people and places made during long visits to Europe, Russia, and the Caribbean have appeared in essays in *The New Yorker* and in two books, *Local Color* (1950) and *The Muses Are Heard* (1956). Born in New Orleans, he spent his boyhood there and in Alabama, his mother's home state. At present he lives in New York.

Capote has devoted his fiction to an examination of the human capacity—or, more often, incapacity—to love. The stunted relationships which he portrays require grotesque characters such as sexual deviates and psychotics to serve as metaphors of the distortion. There are positive relationships which affirm the ability to love, but these are limited to children or to childlike adults. Thwarting the movement toward normal mature love precipitates sinister situations and violence. This frustration may result from the central character's own disturbed psyche, from intolerable pressure brought to bear on a character by an outside force, or, rarely, from the blind course of society toward dullness and complacency. Because the charge against society comes from a child's point of view, it is a complaint of personal dissatisfaction which generally precludes criticism of social issues. There is no expressed awareness of the problems of man in a social context even to the extent to which Goyen is aware, for example, of the decay of community life. Capote himself has explained his approach:

> The content of my work is 'literary'; as opposed, that is, to writing inspired by political or religious convictions, of which I have, in the very orthodox sense, none: so that my source, my point of view, is a matter of private imagination, personal moral beliefs. The 'message' of a story should be after all the story itself.[2]

This preoccupation with the personal sometimes leads Capote close to the precious and the cunningly precocious in his fiction, defects which his technical brilliance cannot disguise. The chief failure which Capote risks is that the horrors of crippled love treated within the narrow limits which he sets finally seem contrived. Then the anguish and violence no longer vivify the fiction.

In dealing with characters unable to love normally, Capote creates monsters more repelling than the subhuman characters of Caldwell's fiction, whose sexuality has at least an animal vigor. Capote's people turn inward with incapacitating self-hatred. Some of the characters are outright insane while others are neurotics partially aware of their problems. Both types appear in "The Headless Hawk." The painter D. J. is a mad young woman fearful of destruction at the hands of a delusion she names Mr. Destronelli. She is befriended by a neurotic art dealer Vincent who can love only the twisted: the

---

2. *Twentieth Century Authors, First Supplement,* ed. Stanley J. Kunitz (New York: The H. W. Wilson Company, 1955), p. 168.

feeble-minded Lucille, the deaf Connie, the homosexual Allen T. Baker—and the insane D. J. Freaks fascinate him, not, he confesses, because he feels sympathy for them, but because they are reflections of himself. In his unease he asks, ". . . oh, why in his loves must he always find the broken image of himself."[3] The disjointedness of his personality is imaged in D. J.'s surrealistic painting of a headless hawk, scarlet and copper, soaring above the figure of a woman whose head lies on the floor, where a kitten plays with the ends of the hair. The fact that he has come to the point of choosing a maniac like D. J. for his mistress forces him to recognize the severity of his own illness, a confrontation with himself which unhinges him.

Internalized violence at times emerges in Capote's fiction as characters who embody abstract evil. Their function is to evoke indefinite fears from which the reader manufactures his own version of evil in much the same way that Henry James on a more complex level frightens his readers with *The Turn of the Screw*. In "A Tree of Night," Kay, a young woman traveling by train, meets a couple who give shows in which the deaf-mute man in a state of self-hypnosis allows himself to be buried alive. The isolation of the mute and the "shocking, embalmed, secret stillness" of his face resemble the dead uncle from whose funeral Kay is returning.[4] Out of Kay's fear of death, her sense of guilt for having rejected her uncle, and the apprehensions aroused by the mute's suggestive caressing of a polished peach stone, Capote concocts an atmosphere more sinister and threatening than the "facts" warrant. Again, the embodiment of evil in Mr. Revercomb, the Master Misery of the story of that title, is frankly allegorical. The shadowy Master Misery buys dreams, but the sellers after a momentary elation lapse into the despair of having irrevocably lost their souls. The spiritual poverty which Mr. Revercomb induces is

3. *A Tree of Night and Other Stories* (New York: Random House, 1949), p. 162.
4. *Ibid.*, p. 203.

a form of the lovelessness which Capote associates with sinister grotesqueness.

The most fully developed wraith of evil in Capote's fiction is the child Miriam in the story which bears her name. As in "A Tree of Night," the personification of evil is a catalytic agent stimulating a presumably innocent character to fear her own internal terrors. Mrs. Miller's inability to cope with Miriam's blandly selfish demands forces the widow to recognize her essential aloneness. Because she cannot endure to lose the identity with which she has masked her real condition, Miriam's presence excites her to hysteria. The reassurance of a neighbor that he cannot find the child in her apartment allows Mrs. Miller to feel "like a diver emerging from some deeper, greener depth."[5] She no longer has to look into the fearful depths of her unconsciousness where her real self lies buried. But there are sounds from the bedroom and Miriam enters. The final horror is that fears from the unassimilated unconscious will not be dismissed.

Capote's master monster is Cousin Randolph of *Other Voices, Other Rooms.* A languid, indolent, overweight, hypochondriacal man in his middle thirties, Randolph has a certain decadent wit and charm. In the course of his subtle campaign to pervert the thirteen-year-old Joel Knox, he bewilders the boy by discussing his rationale for his homosexuality. With the precision of a sensitive intelligence, Randolph describes himself as a man without an interior life who feeds on the energy of others, a non-creative parasite suffering painful guilt for his deviation. He then brings to his defense an argument, which also appears in Carson McCullers' fiction, that any kind of love is acceptable and thus presumably justifies the violence of its practice. The ominous partner in Randolph's schemes is Miss Amy, nurse-wife to Joel's paralyzed father. Often reduced to gibbering idiocy by Randolph's scorn, she has a coldness and cruelty of her own. The third

5. *Ibid.,* p. 133.

grotesque to burden Joel's life at Skully's Landing is the father he had hoped to imitate. Sansom (whose name seems to pun *sans l'homme*) is not the athletic man of Joel's fantasies but a bedridden invalid immobile except for teary eyes and the hand which drops red balls to call for attention. The father with whom Joel should identify himself has literally been destroyed by Randolph, who had shot Sansom in a sordid misunderstanding.

Eventually these three make it impossible for Joel to distinguish between reality and unreality, a distinction he had never lost even when he retired to his inner room of imagination. Capote fully exploits the possibilities for distortion and violence inherent in adolescence in order to portray the obverse of the transition to normal adulthood which Carson McCullers and Eudora Welty present in *Member of the Wedding* and *Delta Wedding*. The violent and the grotesque in Joel's experience is not the tragic-comic exaggeration of Caldwell's characters and plots nor the eccentricities of Goyen's ghosts nor the desperate enlargements of Flannery O'Connor's view of the world; rather it is evil battening on unprotected innocence. Capote heightens the distortion by making its center the family, the institution celebrated in Southern tradition for its solicitude and loyalty.

In treating the grotesqueness and violence of sexual deviation Capote joins other young American writers like Gore Vidal and Frederic Buechner who have experimented with this theme. Henri Peyre points out that the subject was introduced into twentieth-century fiction first by French writers who have since been widely imitated. They were hunting for material with new tragic implications to move audiences jaded by the crises of nineteenth-century realistic fiction.[6] It was inevitable that the freedom which the literary naturalists won to deal with the physiological would be paralleled by an equal freedom to deal with the psychological. When the

6. Henri Peyre, *The Contemporary French Novel* (New York: Oxford University Press, 1955), pp. 32-33.

demarcations of acceptable behavior changed rapidly in the twentieth century, the extreme was a way both to protest the change and to surprise readers. The theme is symptomatic of the hatred of the self and the consequent urge to destroy which has accompanied the disruptions of the twentieth century. Because homosexuality engenders a violence which negates the values held by a healthy society, it has served to express a profound rejection of tradition and order. In exploring this theme in *Other Voices, Other Rooms*, Capote thus shares in a national and an international literary development. In the South he finds the elements of an inimical atmosphere of unwholesomeness and decay to support the perversion of the adolescent Joel.

In his fiction Capote skilfully undergirds the grotesqueness of character and situation by violent actions which are metaphors to express the meaning of the disorder. John W. Aldridge in his analysis of *Other Voices, Other Rooms* identifies the method as metaphorical rather than symbolical because the private psychological elements do not, in his view, transcend themselves to take on larger public moral and ethical meanings.[7] The distinction is a useful one to indicate that the parallels and relations between event and person or between person and person convey a single meaning instead of the multiple meanings which gather into a symbol.

Capote uses the metaphorical method in "The Headless Hawk" when D. J. confuses Vincent with Mr. Destronelli and threatens him with her scissors. Later in an insane frenzy Vincent with a pair of scissors lunges at a butterfly which settles on D. J.'s painting, stabs the hawk, and continues to rip the canvas, thus figuratively killing D. J. and committing suicide. In this way Capote keeps the action of the story on the surrealistic plane already established by the imagery of the painting and the abnormal psychology of the characters. He does not permit the violence to break out of the fictional frame and

7. *After the Lost Generation: A Critical Study of the Writers of Two Wars* (New York: McGraw-Hill Book Company, 1951), p. 203.

enter actuality, where its meaning could no longer be only metaphorical.

That the destructive force which Miriam represents cannot be evaded by refusing to recognize it is made apparent on the child's first visit to Mrs. Miller. Denied a good-night kiss, Miriam smashes a vase containing paper roses against the bare floor and stamps on the bouquet. As the story progresses there is less need for such outward violence because the theme— the terror of having to replace a false identity with a true—is acted out within Mrs. Miller's psyche. Miriam is not really a separate entity, for she betokens the disorder and destruction which are unrealized parts of Mrs. Miller, hence the "cob-webby fingers" with which the child gathers up crumbs.

The abundance of metaphorical correspondences which make *Other Voices, Other Rooms* a total creation has already been noted. Not all of these contain violence, but it is crucial in Joel's relationship with Idabel Thompkins and the Negro servant Zoo, the two people through whom he reaches toward normal maturity. Idabel, the neighborhood tomboy, is, like Joel, struggling to define herself. She is his one opportunity to express an ordinary adolescent attraction to the opposite sex, and her failure to adopt a feminine role becomes part of Joel's failure to trust his masculinity. Her twin Florabel is en-tirely a feminine stereotype, scorned by Idabel and less in-teresting to Joel than the swashbuckling sister. The first time Joel visits the girls they quickly distinguish their attitudes. Florabel carves a heart and initials on the watermelon they are to share; Idabel flashes a jackknife and declares, "I could kill somebody, couldn't I?"[8] She takes part in two fights: the first with Florabel merely illustrates her pugnacity, but the second with Joel is a miniature battle of the sexes in which significantly only Joel is wounded.

In one of their most important sequences together, Idabel's use of violence signifies a fundamental crippling of Joel's

8. *Other Voices, Other Rooms* (New York: Random House, 1948), p. 105.

emotional development. The two prepare to run away, and Joel, wearing a family sword given to him, takes the lead. As they cross the creek on a board, Joel is transfixed by the sight of a coiled cottonmouth moccasin. The eyes of the snake recall those of his father. Feelings of guilt for having denied his father immobilize him. Idabel thrusts the boy behind her and with his sword kills the snake. Thus she betrays both Joel and herself by usurping his masculine prerogative and by rejecting her feminine dependence. Capote later introduces Miss Wisteria, a midget with a carnival, who is for Idabel the grotesque equivalent of Cousin Randolph in Joel's life.

The violence which has disfigured Zoo frightens Joel away from the outside world. The first time Joel sees the scar on Zoo's throat left by her husband's attempt to murder her, he is horrified. He rushes into a briarpatch as if seeking pain to disprove his uncertainty. After her ancient grandfather dies, Zoo sets out for Washington, D. C., to fulfil her dreams of happiness. For Joel this trip is also his escape, but Zoo returns with nothing but a report of violations. She had been held at the point of a gun and raped by white men. Hearing about these events while he is convalescing from a serious fever is more than Joel can endure. He rejects the ugliness and the pain and with them the mixed conditions of the world outside the Landing.

Violence which a child cannot understand is an essential part of the process of weakening Joel so that he will become unnaturally dependent upon Randolph. His capture, which is adumbrated by Miss Amy's cornering and killing a bluejay in Joel's bedroom on the boy's first morning at the Landing, is completed during the novel. And the hawk shot at the moment Joel discovered that his letters to friends in the real world were not being mailed foretells the psychological death which abnormal love will bring him.

The inert, static, and sterile existence at Skully's Landing connotes the emotional vacuum of life in the twentieth century and the paralysis of will which plagues man. If the novel sees only a small part of human nature, it is still symptomatic of a contemporary malaise. Further evidence of the moral exhaustion of the century is the fact that the author reacts to the waste of Joel's life with regret rather than outrage. But the monstrous decadence of Randolph is none the less sinister. Because the story is told through Joel, who only imperfectly realizes the significance of the steps in his perversion, it has the pathos and poignancy of immaturity and unawareness, although it lacks the compelling dignity and pity of tragedy.

When Capote moves into his fictional world where characters have a capacity for normal love, the tone changes. The dissonance instead of being sinister becomes obliquely merry. The exaggeration of character and situation is fanciful and generally points toward a creative imaginative life. The world and its people are again largely juvenile.

The absurdly adult ten-year-old Miss Lily Jane Bobbit in "Children on Their Birthdays" is a precocious creature of Capote's imagination, whose behavior is entirely metaphorical. "I think always about somewhere else," she explains, "somewhere else where everything is dancing, like people dancing in the streets, and everything is pretty, like children on their birthdays."[9] Her irruption into a small town represents everything that is not mediocre, routine, and dully middle class.

The harmless insanity of Miss Dolly Talbo in *The Grass Harp* performs the same function as Miss Bobbit's more aggressive attack on bourgeois respectability. The grotesqueness of the situation in the novel is playfully fantastic although the details are as realistic as the everyday world. Dolly's domineering and practical sister Verena, already wealthy and the center of family gossip, wants to make more money. Dolly thwarts the scheme by refusing to reveal her recipe for a dropsy cure which Verena and a promoter want to market commercially. In the ensuing disagreement, Dolly feels obliged to leave home. Catherine Creek, her addled Negro-

9. *A Tree of Night*, p. 49.

Indian companion, and Collin Fenwick, her sixteen-year-old cousin, come with her to a tree house. When Charlie Cool, a retired judge, and Riley Henderson, young man about town, join the trio, the "five fools in a tree," as the Judge labels them, discourse on love. The Judge's theory "that love is a chain of love, as nature is a chain of life" runs throughout the novel.[10] The only people capable of living by this principle are the innocent, hence the combination of childlike age, pleasant insanity, and youth among the characters.

In *Breakfast at Tiffany's* Capote again treats the theme of the search for love the abnormal. This time the combination of playfulness and violence fails to achieve the happy urgency which it has in *The Grass Harp*. Holly's rural origin as Lulamae Barnes and her escape to New York from a doting husband and step-children whom she acquired when she was fourteen presumably account for the traces of naïveté and wistfulness which distinguish her from ordinary urban sophisticates. Her waywardness remains pure caprice. Whatever she might have learned about how to recognize the things she wants before she throws them away is lost in her flightiness, which is childish rather than childlike. Holly is too innocent to be grotesque, but she is accompanied by grotesques like the infantile playboy Rusty Trawler and the stuttering lesbian May Wildwood. She protects or uses such people at her whim; she is not significantly related to them. Most of the violence in her life which might have helped to define her character leaves her untouched. For all of her lack of inhibitions, Holly is coolly in control of herself. Her single great outburst of personal violence is the wrecking of her apartment to express her grief at the loss of her brother, the one person whose love she has fully trusted. Living a fly-by-night existence, staging boisterous parties, stealing for the thrill of escaping, and dabbling in the gangster world of illegal trade in narcotics are activities which seem manufactured for Holly. She does not finally take on the fictional reality of an inner-

10. *The Grass Harp* (New York: Random House, 1951), p. 75.

motivated character or a creature of fantasy like Dolly Talbo. The people who inhabit Capote's dark world gain credibility from the sheer suggestive power of wickedness, but those in his light world verge toward the sentimental when the humor subsides.

Among the stories in which the capacity for love has some positive expression, violence figures most significantly in "Children on Their Birthdays" and *The Grass Harp*. Miss Bobbit's actions provide a genial critique of Southern bourgeois culture. At one point Capote delivers an explicit criticism through violence. Miss Bobbit rescues a Negro girl from abusive boys and keeps her as a companion addressed as "sister." Alarmed townspeople protest, but they gradually come to look on the eccentricity as natural. With Miss Bobbit, Capote slyly reverses the traditional Southern assumption that country ways are preferable to city manners. Her sophistication finally charms the town into accepting Miss Bobbit as proof that pleasure is not incompatible with morality and that aestheticism may be more sensitive to injustice than is moralism.

The outrage of the middle class when convention and profits are challenged is exemplified in *The Grass Harp* by the attack which the townspeople launch to bring Dolly and her defenders down to earth. Shouted epithets, gouging, kicking, and sly trickery in an attenuated version of fights such as those portrayed by Southwest humorists make up the siege. The violence and the humor are augmented by the appearance of Sister Ida, an itinerant evangelist who roams the country in a wagon filled with her eleven children, including Texaco Gasoline and Little Homer. The latter lassos the Reverend Buster and precipitates an all-out bombardment by his brothers and sisters. Church and town are defeated and the sisters are reconciled.

The oddities of the characters in this novel and the poetizing on love are preserved from becoming excessively sentimental only by the framework of fantasy and the humor of the violence. The realism of the created fantastic episode is kept wholly separate from the commonplace, and is never broken by the intrusion of incongruous passion, anxiety, failure, or other contingencies which disrupt ordinary life. But the escape thus provided is so pure that the reader has little to bring back with him.

In another piece of light grotesquerie, "My Side of the Matter," the elements of exaggeration create a topsy-turvy humor reminiscent of that in Eudora Welty's "Why I Live at the P. O." The first-person narrator is an amiable paranoiac who thrives on extreme emotions. Capote sketches this character for the sake of his amusing personality alone without the background network of family and community relationships against which Miss Welty exhibits her postmistress. The spinster aunts likewise are treated only for the humor of Eunice's uncouthness and obesity and of dim-witted Olivia-Ann's pleasure in whittling with a fourteen-inch hog knife. The facts which might develop into ugliness or painful distortion are deflected into mere curiosities, and the battle between the narrator and the aunts is a *Joseph Andrews* mock-epic conflict seen through the large end of a telescope. The violence makes the participants ridiculous without revealing character or culture in the robust manner of Faulkner or Caldwell.

The technical virtuosity of Capote makes him more consequential than do his ideas. Overwritten passages, which occur more frequently in *Other Voices, Other Rooms* than in the later work, are likely to be hypersensitive descriptions of moods and sensations. For the most part, Capote adroitly makes language perform as he wishes. His chief art is the creation of external parallels for highly subjective states of feeling. When these states arise from abnormalities of personality or of human relationships, they reflect Capote's view of the dark side of man. It is at this point that the ugly, foreboding, sinister aspects of the grotesque and the threatening and unsettling aspects of violence appear. They may be conveyed in direct description, such as that which sets the lonesome, stagnant swamp country background for *Other Voices, Other Rooms,* but most frequently Capote depends upon characterization and situation, particularly a situation which would appear perfectly normal to someone on the outside: a painter brings her work to an art gallery, a young boy goes to visit his father, a child calls on a widow. When Capote turns to the positive side of man reaching toward affirmative relationships, the grotesque and the violent lighten and become amusing. The exaggerations may be just as extreme as they are in the stories of crippled love, but they are not destructive.

The fact that Capote deals with these approaches in separate compartments severely limits his vision. The limitation suggests the dissociated sensibility which Jung has analyzed as the primary problem of modern man. In this respect, violence and grotesqueness in Capote's work are more representative of the situation of man in the world as a whole than in Southern culture alone. This extension of meaning, however, does not inhere in the fiction itself but must be drawn from outside. Because Capote is chiefly interested in almost purely psychological problems without their moral dimensions, distortions of the psyche are presented for their sake alone. Recognition of the disorder is more important to him than judgment on it, and his portrayals imply that acceptance of disordered lives is the proper response. The sense of the tragic disparity between what man is and what fate requires of him which directs Faulkner's thought is exchanged in Capote's work for a tentative hope that man might be spared judgment for being what he is. This attitude undercuts the reader's reaction to the violent and the grotesque and reduces their shock potential, but it increases their value as serious indicators of the degree to which the agony of man has become private.

VII. Dispossessed love: Carson McCullers

The motif of Carson Smith McCullers' fiction is love, its modes, demands, successes, defeats, grace, and shame. Whatever force, instinct, or need holds the human community together, this is love. The falling apart of the community is signaled by the breakdown of communications between persons, by physical and spiritual isolation, by hatred and fear, by sexual perversion, or by economic and racial injustice, and violence accompanies all negations. Within each negation, however, there is a drive toward a positive alliance. No matter how distorted the relationship may be, Mrs. McCullers has compassion for every attempt of the human being to become a *we* instead of an *I*, as the adolescent heroine of *The Member of the Wedding* puts the problem. Thus the author is charitable toward the violence and grotesqueness which develop when the impulse to love goes astray, and she treats deviations more with mercy than with horror. This mercy, however, is less rigorous than that expressed by Flannery O'Connor. Mrs. McCullers feels sympathy for the yearning of her characters for something better than the confusion into which they have fallen. Miss O'Connor feels compassion for characters because as human beings they suffer bodily and spiritual deformities. Their misery, in fact, is an inevitable consequence of their humanity. Mrs. McCullers, on the other hand, sees the derangement of human life as a passing failure to be solved by a human restoration of beneficial relationships. Violence in her fiction therefore lacks the inexorable moral toughness present in the work of Miss O'Connor.

Despite the prevalence of conflict, frustration, grief, pain, and fear in Mrs. McCullers' work, the mood is seldom morbid or bitterly melancholy. Although the characters suffer grotesque physical or psychological disfigurement, they struggle toward meaning, even though it may never come. The sense of nothingness and despair which at times overwhelms the characters of William Goyen and Truman Capote also visits her people, but they project the feeling into some form of violence. The suffering, then, instead of being brooded over is acted out in fighting, murder, or mutilation, or is spoken out in vehement arguments.

The South which Mrs. McCullers uses is made up of the lower and middle economic strata in small cities or in hamlets: petty bourgeoisie who own cafés or jewelry shops; cotton mill workers, oppressed by long hours and inadequate wages; Negroes—professional men and servants—whose wisdom and patience are only partially available to either black or white. Their environment includes long glaring summers of heat and short changeable winters, drab houses and odors of poverty, blocks of shops, offices, and factories; and streets where faces have "the desperate look of hunger and of loneliness."[1] Occasionally there are flashes of the red cotton land and black pine woods beyond the towns. The prevailing bleak ugliness accords with the violence of the lives traced by Mrs. McCullers, a use of Southern locale similar to that of Flannery O'Connor.

A native of Columbus, Georgia, where she was born in 1917, Mrs. McCullers sets most of her fiction in places which could be duplicated in Columbus or the neighboring countryside. Although the theme of dispossessed love unifies all of her work, the circumstances for its development vary so widely as to seem new and original in each book. In her first novel, *The Heart Is a Lonely Hunter* (1940), the troubles of a mill town shadow the thwarted loves. The following year she published *Reflections in a Golden Eye*, an account of a murder at

1. *The Heart Is a Lonely Hunter* (Boston: Houghton Mifflin Company, 1940), p. 6.

an army post in the South augmented in horror by the diseased bodies and minds of the characters. *The Member of the Wedding* (1946) sympathetically presented the shocks and violence endured by an imaginative adolescent trying to understand her maturing personality. This novel was successfully dramatized in 1950 and won the Donaldson Award and the New York Drama Critics Prize. In 1951 the three novels were collected with a novella, *The Ballad of the Sad Café*, and six short stories in a volume published under the title of the novella. During the following decade she published short pieces and in 1961 another novel, *Clock Without Hands*. In her fiction violence and distortion are parts of the often frightening labyrinthine complexity of love. Fear, infidelity, anger, and violence frequently overcome her characters long before they have found any passage through the labyrinth. Mrs. McCullers portrays the full terror of these defeats, but she never adopts the introspective morbidity of the defeated.

Love as a relationship which permits genuine communication between persons is the goal of most of Mrs. McCullers' characters. Thus the goal in itself represents nothing violent or distorted, but thwarting its achievement inevitably destroys order in both the outer and the inner worlds. One of the primary images of the difficulty of reaching across the barriers between even kindly disposed people appears in *The Heart Is a Lonely Hunter*, where it unifies theme and structure. At the center of the novel John Singer, a deaf-mute, like the hub of a wheel receives four spokes of the narrative in the stories of Jake Blount, a labor reformer; Benedict Copeland, a Negro doctor and educator; Mick Kelly, an adolescent girl with a gift for composing music; and Biff Brannon, the sexually ambivalent owner of a restaurant. Each of these has his separate violence which he brings to Singer's quiet acceptance: Jake's rage at economic injustice, Copeland's anger at the servitude of his people, Mick's adolescent tensions, and Biff's emotional frustrations. But when the four people meet in Singer's rooms, each maintains his isolation. Singer had expected a violent encounter, "but in the room there was only a feeling of strain. His hands worked nervously as though they were pulling things unseen from the air and binding them together."[2] Although the four become involved with one another outside Singer's room, they remain suspicious and uncertain. They are caught in a perverse rejection of their own good, the same perversity which Flannery O'Connor depicts in young Tarwater when the social welfare worker tries to remove the boy from his old uncle's care.[3] Their refusal is repeated by other characters. Loneliness is as inescapable in Mrs. McCullers' fictional world as it is in that of Eudora Welty or William Goyen.

The anguish and fear to which loneliness subjects human beings may be contained within the words of a tortured spirit or it may erupt into violence and antisocial behavior. For the unnamed man in the café in "A Tree. A Rock. A Cloud" who talks to a bewildered paper boy, words rather than acts describe the wildness of his search for an unfaithful wife and the resolution of his sorrow in learning to love by beginning with a tree, a rock, or a cloud, a design also recommended by Judge Cool in *The Grass Harp*. Madame Zilensky ("Madame Zilensky and the King of Finland") lies boldly in order to have a life which she can share with others, and Mr. Brook, who once tried to force his colleague to admit her outrageous exaggerations, feels that he has attempted to murder her. Children are especially vulnerable to a breach in the confidence they have established with adults. In their defenselessness they may strike out to inflict a reciprocal injury. Hugh Harris ("The Haunted Boy") is tortured by the memory of having found his mother after she had cut her wrists. After her recovery he remains anxious, and when she forgets to leave a note explaining why she will not be at home when Hugh returns from school, he reacts with hysterical anger and fear.

The sickening sweep into the oblivion of complete isolation

2. *Ibid.*, p. 208.
3. Flannery O'Connor, *The Violent Bear It Away*, p. 181.

is one of the constituents of violence which Mrs. McCullers portrays with special effectiveness. The consequences of a broken trust may be violent enough to change the personality of a character. After Bubber Kelley impulsively shoots Baby Wilson, Mick mistakenly tries to discipline her brother by frightening him with talk of Sing Sing, electric chairs which fry children like bacon, and consignment to hell, threats actually prompted by a love which desires to keep Bubber dependent upon her. But the boy runs away and when brought home withdraws into sullen apathy so that he is never again youthful in his ways. His wounding Baby Wilson was less a shock than was the willingness of Mick to turn his violence and fear into a weapon against him.

Among adults the fear of loneliness ignites violent reactions. Although Captain Penderton in *Reflections in a Golden Eye* is more enamored of his wife's lovers than of his wife, he is frightened by the possibility of being left alone should Leonora's current lover win a divorce. The Captain's need to hate is as acute as his need to love, for only in the polarity of these emotions can he feel secure against solitude. Once Penderton becomes absorbed in trying to establish a relationship with the country soldier Ellgee Williams, he is hypersensitive to his own isolation. Nothing that he observes has meaning except in connection with his peculiar needs. He thinks of violence as a way to attract Williams by shouting at him or striking him. The violent impulses of Williams, on the other hand, set him off as an entirely non-reflective counterpart of the brooding Captain: "The mind of Private Williams was imbued with various colors of strong tones, but it was without delineation, void of form."[4] In anger he had once killed a Negro and secretly buried him; in the excitement of desire for Leonora whom he watches at night, he often stirs up fights in the barracks. Entirely absorbed in sensation, he is incapable of naming to himself the violence in which he engages.

4. *Reflections in a Golden Eye* (Boston: Houghton Mifflin Company, 1941), p. 131.

The defense which another lonely man—Singer—chooses after the death of his fellow mute Antonapoulos is suicide. Singer intends this violence as a ritual of friendship, a tribute to their companionship. To the others who had depended upon him the suicide is a betrayal which leaves them further isolated. So overpowering is the need to share human loneliness that the townspeople had elevated Singer into a kind of deity by virtue of his affliction. It seemed to make him uncanny, and it allowed each man to describe the mute "as he wished to be."[5] Singer himself in turn deified Antonapoulos, treating the fat man's self-indulgence like the whim of a classical god and attributing to him the wisdom of a Buddha. The violence which seems resolved in Singer points to the ironic fact that man fashions God after his own image. For Mrs. McCullers, then, the violence which dwells with loneliness is finally the absence of any real god; for Miss O'Connor it is the presence of the God.

Although Mrs. McCullers often portrays adults as physically and emotionally ruined people, she brings her adolescents through violence to a healthy measure of maturity. This ability to achieve wholeness distinguishes their growth from that of many young people in twentieth-century literature about the suffering adolescent. The struggle of the adolescent who appears in the fiction of William Goyen or Truman Capote injures or defeats him with a deadly finality. Mrs. McCullers prefers to educate rather than to destroy her adolescents with violence.

Mick Kelly, although more gifted than Frankie Addams, her counterpart in *The Member of the Wedding,* is less given to introspective analysis and to confusing actual events with her fantasies of them. For Mick the initiation into adulthood includes unpleasant facts like a summer job that probably means the end of her formal education and the draining off of the energy which had shaped music in her mind. The responsibilities of a child in a poor family keep Mick from indulging

5. *The Heart Is a Lonely Hunter,* p. 221.

in the violence for which Frankie has both the leisure and the imagination. Mick has painted her sense of a violent world in pictures of storms, city fires, airplane crashes, and battling citizens. This violence invades her home when she gives a prom. Neighborhood children crash into the scene and set off a general regression to juvenile behavior. The final melee epitomizes adolescent flightiness. This debacle, a structural parallel for the fight in which Jack is later involved, is one of the concluding ceremonies of Mick's adolescence. It does not, however, end her development.

In her study of Frankie Addams, Mrs. McCullers focuses on the violence of the conflicting irrational drives which frighten the girl. On impulse Frankie has stolen a knife, has shot off her father's pistol in town, and has committed what she calls a secret sin with Barney MacKean. She threatens to knife the Negro cook Berenice and alternately courts and repels her young cousin John Henry. Mrs. McCullers makes clear that the violence which touches Frankie comes not merely from the tomboyish exuberance of a healthy animal but also from the hidden, increasingly devious desires of a maturing human being. The edge of the sinister hangs over Frankie's encounter with a drunk soldier and her escape from his room, but the child does not enter fully into its meaning: "There slanted across her mind twisted remembrances of a common fit in the front room, basement remarks, and nasty Barney; but she did not let these separate glimpses fall together, and the word she repeated was 'crazy.' "[6]

The wedding as symbol in this novel is directly related to the growth of a single central figure. By contrast, in Eudora Welty's *Delta Wedding* the marriage of a Fairchild daughter is the author's occasion for portraying the whole structure of a Southern family. For Frankie the marriage of her brother is to provide her a new relationship of permanent love and security. Her fantasies preceding the wedding and her tantrum

---

6. *The Member of the Wedding* (Boston: Houghton Mifflin Company, 1946), p. 165.

when she is prevented from joining the couple on their honey-moon are the last expressions of an infantile possessiveness. After this scene, both her childishness and her overreaching attempts to be adult are reconciled in the girl who now calls herself *Frances* and who has again found a close friend and schoolgirl enthusiasms.

The girl's passage from childhood to youth is neatly sum-marized in the forms of her names which she adopts: the *Frankie* of her childish past, the *F. Jasmine* of her daydreams of growing up, and the *Frances* of her developing maturity. Each stage has its appropriate violence: the boisterous ram-pages of Frankie, the irresponsible boldness and theatrically threatened suicide of F. Jasmine, and the briefly suggested infatuations of Frances. There is a remarkable balance be-tween the emotional sensitivity of the child and the intel-lectual immaturity which cannot comprehend her experi-ences. Frankie never becomes a precocious monster. She leans over the rim of disaster but genuine innocence prevents her from toppling.

Although changed by the violence she experiences, Frances is not injured by it and crippled emotionally as is Joel Knox in *Other Voices, Other Rooms*, nor disoriented as is the young narrator of *The House of Breath*. Nothing in her Southern en-vironment has been irrevocably menacing; in fact, the naïveté and simplicity of her culture seem positive supports in com-parison with the pressures of egocentric isolation and sophisti-cation in the world of J. D. Salinger's Holden Caufield. Hol-den's violence is artificial and imitative, aping the pretentious ennui of the adults around him. His displacement is more rad-ical than Frankie's because his society has no place for him, whereas the community of Frankie or of Mick, less large and competitive, defines what is acceptable in the stages through which the girls grow and also superintends their progress. The presence of a social pattern, such as the family or the com-munity to which the adolescent is related, checks the violence which occurs in the development of young characters in the fiction of Southern writers like Mrs. McCullers and Eudora Welty. In one short story, "A Domestic Dilemma," Mrs. McCullers makes the removal of the structure of Southern life contribute to domestic violence. Transplanted to New York, Emily disintegrates without the matrix of family and friends to provide a context for her life. The weaknesses which Emily would have controlled had she been filling a place in a known social structure break out as alcoholism and neglect of her children. Her husband Martin sees nothing ahead but "degradation and slow ruin."[7]

If the adolescents in Mrs. McCullers' novels escape psychic injuries, the adults are not so fortunate. The force of strong emotions—whether normal or abnormal, all are forms of love in Mrs. McCullers' view—has warped many of her characters. Furthermore, she often uses disfigured bodies and impaired minds to underscore all that is problematic in human relations. Such hazards become proofs of the incomprehensible perversity of love in which the mutually repellent are not only attracted to one another but also are held together in unlikely relationships. This theme is explicitly developed in *The Ballad of the Sad Café* when repressed, mannish, managerial Miss Amelia falls in love with Cousin Lymon, a shriveled hunchback, and the hunchback in turn bestows his affection on Marvin Macy, a handsome rake who loves and marries Miss Amelia. The circle of pursuing and fleeing lovers repeats the wheel figures indicative of human separateness in *The Heart Is a Lonely Hunter*. The violence which attends the revolution of this charged circle in *The Ballad of the Sad Café* develops in the direct manner of folk literature which the title promises. Like an image of her spirit of pleasure which Miss Amelia had distorted through greed and violent litigiousness, the misshapen cousin quickly restores geniality, courtesy, and graciousness to the dreary mill town by turning Miss Amelia's store into a café. And like an embodiment of Loki, he is also

7. *The Ballad of the Sad Café* (Boston: Houghton Mifflin Company, 1951), p. 26.

the principle of disorder in the midst of order; for "when he walked into the room there was always a quick feeling of tension, because with this busybody about there was never any telling what might descend on you, or what might suddenly be brought to happen in the room."[8] The conflict of affections among the principals quickly foments a fight like a match between folk heroes as Miss Amelia and Macy hammer at one another. Cousin Lymon breaks Miss Amelia's heart by aiding Macy and going off with him after the two wreck her house. The waddling figure of the hunchback dragging his green shawl after him and nibbling a mixture of cocoa and sugar to sweeten his sour teeth intensifies the conflict by making the attachments seem strangely arbitrary and grotesque. In the tradition of the ballad there are no explanations for erratic behavior which without motive disrupts the expected quiet and provokes the unexpected violence.

Freaks serve Mrs. McCullers as illustrations of the attraction-repulsion equation. Frankie Addams fears the possibility of ugliness in herself, an ugliness which she believes is implied by the connection the carnival freaks seem to establish with her. Biff Brannon, on the other hand, is fascinated by all the maimed, diseased, and misshapen who come to his café. The compassion which he expresses in his generosity to them is an extension of the human community, an affirmation of the author's belief that man in all conditions merits dignified treatment. Outward deformity in Mrs. McCuller's characters is not simply a reflection of twisted inner lives to express a tragic vision of life as Dayton Kohler proposes.[9] Instead, Mrs. McCullers stresses the accidental rather than the inevitable nature of this condition; it is one of the chances of life that shows up love for the paradox of violence and calm, gentleness and cruelty, beauty and ugliness which it is. The lives of the physically afflicted like Cousin Lymon or John Singer contain their private tragedies of isolation and despair, but

8. *Ibid.*, p. 37.
9. "Carson McCullers: Variations on a Theme," *English Journal*, XL (Oct., 1951), 417.

they also generate love and restrain violence. Within themselves and in the relationship of others to them they have an
effect similar to Miss Amelia's liquor: it causes joy and suffering but it reveals the truth and warms the soul.

When the capacity for love has been utterly twisted, the
result is the grotesqueness and violence of perversion and an
aggregation of misery such as confounds the characters in
Reflections in a Golden Eye. Penderton's homosexuality, sad-
ism, and masochism destroy him as effectively as he destroys
those around him. His psychological deterioration is matched
by physical disintegration. His complexion yellows, his teeth
ache, and his left eyelid twitches in a tic which "gave to his
face a strangely paralyzed expression."[10] Like Cousin Randolph in *Other Voices, Other Rooms* he maintains that abnormality is not immorality, but he has a sickening vision of
himself, "a distorted doll-like image, mean of countenance
and grotesque in form."[11] In murdering the soldier Williams,
Penderton kills the animal energy that alternately frightens
and fascinates him. The way to this final violence is marked
by psychotic behavior like the brutal beating by which Penderton breaks the spirit of a riding horse, the exhibitionism
of Leonora, and the self-mutilation and near madness of Ali-
son. Absorbed in their violence, the characters never recognize its cause. They act out the psychological depravity of
man when the impulse to love has been fatally thwarted.
Penderton's failure is tenuously linked to the efforts of five
old-maid aunts to make him a "southern gentleman," but the
phrase appears too casually to imply any real connection between it as cause and Penderton as result. Where Faulkner
creates character by a complex meshing of history, geography,
and psychology, Mrs. McCullers in this novel draws chiefly
on psychology, simplifying characters to case studies. Their
private violence against themselves and their associates is
clinical.

10. *Reflections in a Golden Eye*, p. 155.
11. *Ibid.*, p. 163.

Violence which flares when characters clash with social institutions functions as social criticism. For Jake Blount in *The
Heart Is a Lonely Hunter* labor agitation and reform express
the general love for mankind which racks his body and spirit
until he gives the impression of being deformed. His extreme
responses verge on insanity. When drunk and frustrated, he
beats his head against a wall; when hungry, he names over
foods with the lifted lip of a ravenous animal; when amused,
he laughs like a maniac. With the temperament and zeal of a
martyr, he had devoted himself to religion, but when he was
converted to the cause of labor he became a prophet of reform. Despite his thorough secularization, Jake is grotesquely
marred by his religious anger; he carries the scar of a nail he
once drove through his hand. Years later when he is challenged by a street preacher, he shocks the old man by showing
him this travesty of the stigmata. The violence discharged by
Jake's energy suggests the ease with which undisciplined
emotion degenerates into disorder.

Jake as reformer represents a modern form of sentimentality
in which the excess of emotion is violent rather than soft-
hearted. He speaks a philosophy based on the theories of Marx
and Veblen, but his drive comes from a heart touched by the
mean life of those whose work is someone else's profit. The
exuberance of his habits and the fierceness of his talk create
the effect of violence even when Jake is not stirring up trouble.
Mrs. McCullers is not concerned to make his intellectual position credible but to portray again the force, both destructive
and constructive, of another form of love. The violence of
Jake's reaching out to the oppressed shocks his hearers. To
the men in the café he introduces himself in a Whitmanesque
swagger: "I'm part nigger and wop and bohunk and chink. . . .
And I'm Dutch and Turkish and Japanese and American."[12]
Despite this declaration, he suffers the alienation which Mrs.

12. *The Heart Is a Lonely Hunter*, p. 23.

McCullers finds inevitable in the human paradox. He admits, "I'm a stranger in a strange land."[13]

When the burden of separation and the uneasiness of thwarted love grows excessive, Mrs. McCullers' chief device for releasing the tension is a fight. In *The Heart Is a Lonely Hunter* this explosion involves not just the private emotions of the principal figures as it does in *The Ballad of the Sad Café,* but the disaffections of the entire community. Mrs. McCullers builds toward the climax of violence by moving from the periphery of action to Jake's involvement. During the slack winter the unrest of the mill people breaks out in evangelical fervor, in racial hatred, and in murder. In the spring Jake finds the body of a murdered Negro. On his job at the Sunny Dixie Show he notices frequent fights and quarrels. He senses that "beneath the gaudy gaiety of the show, the bright lights, and the lazy laughter," there is "something sullen and dangerous."[14] When conflict between a Negro and a white boy triggers a fight throughout the carnival crowd, Jake plunges in. Mrs. McCullers springs the accumulated tensions of the novel in the shock of body against body, hard fists against wet mouths. Like a Hemingway hero, Jake relishes the brutality and the absorption of his power into elemental action. Although he must leave the city under suspicion of having instigated the fight, he goes with hope that he can begin again to do something about the poverty of the South. It is significant that Mrs. McCullers does not involve Jake in a strike at the mills, for the violence which interests her is that of the individual personality rather than that of economic and social systems, such as Steinbeck, Farrell, and Caldwell portrayed in novels published during the depression. In this respect her treatment of violence in relation to social criticism in Southern fiction is a transitional step between the more nearly doctrinaire approach of a writer like Caldwell and the indirectness of William Goyen.

13. *Ibid.*
14. *Ibid.*, p. 284.

One aspect of violence in the social structure of the South, however, occupies Mrs. McCullers more fully than it does other writers in this group, except Faulkner. She treats the conflicts among Negroes and between Negroes and whites with sensitive comprehension and sympathy. The difficulties of the educated Negro who longs to improve the status of his people complicate the life of Dr. Benedict Copeland. Misunderstanding which leads to violence within Dr. Copeland's own family reveals the numerous but conflicting ways in which a Negro may establish his self-respect. Copeland himself chose austerity and intense study, but his wild bouts of despair had alienated his wife and children. His father-in-law believes that the race problem will be solved only at the Last Judgment when the black are made white. This view of their future rather than the Marxist theories and scholarship of their father shapes the Copeland children. The sons are ordinary workmen, accepting most of the stereotypes of race; the daughter Portia is a cook for a white family.

The Negroes, it is evident, will meet white people chiefly in two relations: domestic employment and law enforcement, and it is in the latter, of course, that they are most likely to be involved in violence. Two young Negro men, Honey in *The Member of the Wedding* and Willie in *The Heart Is a Lonely Hunter,* commit offenses for which they are imprisoned. Berenice, the Addams' cook, tries to explain to Frankie why Negroes sometimes run berserk:

Everybody is caught one way or another. But they done drawn completely extra bounds around all colored people. They done squeezed us off in one corner by ourself. So we caught that first way I was telling you, as all human beings is caught. And we caught as colored people also. Sometimes it just about more than we can stand.[15]

This frustration motivates Lancy Davis, a Negro high school student in *The Heart Is a Lonely Hunter,* who writes an essay on the subject "My Ambition: How I Can Better the Position

15. *The Member of the Wedding,* p. 144.

of the Negro Race in Society." Because he does not want to "sow where others reap," he envisions a revolution: "I hate the whole white race and will work always so that the colored race can achieve revenge for all their sufferings."[16] Ironically, Lancy is one of the Negroes killed in the racial clash at the Sunny Dixie Show. Mrs. McCullers' account of the way white officials treat Negroes is even more brutal than Caldwell's. Prison guards shut Willie in an ice locker room, where his feet freeze so that they must later be amputated. Deputy sheriffs beat and jail Dr. Copeland when he fails to play Uncle Remus at the courthouse. Violence in these instances is the white man's instrument for maintaining his authority, and the Negro's answer in violence has no power because it is a solitary assault on consolidated officialdom. Dr. Copeland, in fact, later speaks of the South as a fascist country in which Negroes endure the same loss of privilege as Jews in Nazi Germany. "The history of my people," he prophesies, "will be commensurate with the interminable history of the Jew—only bloodier and more violent."[17]

Other psychological complexities of any meeting between Negro and white appear in *Clock Without Hands*. The adolescent Negro Sherman Pew, who embodies a century of hate, is a person to only one of the three white people whose lives touch his in Milan, Georgia. To aging Judge Fox Clane, Sherman as the son of the white woman once loved by Clane's son, is a reminder of the hopes lost when the young lawyer Johnny Clane committed suicide. To J. T. Malone, a pharmacist dying of leukemia, Sherman is a strange nigger whose blue eyes blaze with an "eerie understanding" that the white man will soon die. To Jester, the Judge's grandson, Sherman is a first friend who could share music and poetry with him but holds him off with lies and rudeness. The story of the social revolution which even the Judge admits is occurring in the South and the story of Malone's final search for answers run parallel

16. *The Heart Is a Lonely Hunter*, p. 181.
17. *Ibid.*, p. 297.

without illuminating one another except in the moment when Malone refuses to kill Sherman in the plot of the "ragtag and bobtail" citizens to remove the Negro from the house which he rents on the fringe of a white neighborhood. "I am too near death to sin, to murder," Malone explains.[18] No considerations of the possible immortality of his soul deter Sammy Lank, who tosses a bomb at the throat of Sherman who is playing his installment-bought piano and singing.

The violence of the adults in this novel carries forward the customary stereotypes, but the relation of Jester and Sherman points in a new direction. Jester's unexplained desire to treat Sherman as an equal may be the result of a moral evolution which will eventually eliminate color barriers. With a naïveté not credible in a seventeen-year-old, Jester expects Sherman to trust his overtures, and he takes the rebuffs without malice. He is faithful to a Sherman who warns him not to have the "least lewd lascivious thought about Cinderella Mullins," who hangs his dog, who "vibrate[s] with every injustice that is done to my race."[19] Surrounded by violence in the suicide of his father whom he never saw, in the belligerence of his grandfather, in the death of the feeble-minded Negro Grown Boy killed on a Milan street by a blow from a policeman, in the bombing of Sherman, and in his own intention to kill Sammy Lank, Jester nevertheless feels compassion. In the author's omniscient view, Jester has been touched by pity and sorrow, so that presumably he will always refuse to act with the sudden violences of his predecessors. He will learn to look into the eyes of an enemy with love. In him the Judge's fear, Malone's despair, and Sherman's hatred will be resolved. Because this hope proceeds chiefly from statements in the novel, it does not persuade with the certainty which love carries in the dramatized realizations in Mrs. McCullers' earlier novels.

The meeting between Negroes and whites as persons, however, can be constructive. Negro servants may manage white

18. *Clock Without Hands* (Boston: Houghton Mifflin Company, 1961), p. 224.
19. *Ibid.*, pp. 73, 83.

households. Berenice and Portia, for example, are surrogate parents who direct and train the children in their care. They serve as confidantes and set standards for manners, courtesy, and behavior which curb the violence of adolescents like Frankie Addams and Mick Kelly. Sympathetic with the girls who are torn by innumerable conflicting interests and emotions, the Negro women nonetheless sharply censure the violent, irresponsible behavior which the families ignore or dismiss. Both cooks are aware that uneasiness and violence spring from a lack of love. Portia lectures Mick:

> But you haven't never loved God nor even nair person. You hard and tough as cowhide.... This afternoon you going to roam all over the place without never being satisfied.... You going to work yourself up with excitement. Your heart going to beat hard enough to kill you because you don't love and don't have peace. And then some day you going to bust loose and be ruined.[20]

In the same manner by reminiscing about her four marriages Berenice indirectly instructs Frankie in the need for love even in the violent form of Berenice's husband who became insane or the one who gouged out her eye. These dialogues make it possible for Frankie to identify herself with the mature woman instead of with the child John Henry. Berenice is even less a servant and more an adult of the family than is Portia, a fact indicated by the conflict between Frankie and Berenice. The vehemence of their exchanges and Frankie's threats are part of the struggle of equals. Both Negro women, indeed, are fully dimensioned characters who, although their families suffer violence from whites, remain loyal and strong for the whites who depend upon them. Their reactions are more complex than those of a character like Julia Peterkin's Gullah Sister Mary in *Scarlet Sister Mary*, but they accept love and disaster with a similar unquestioning assent.

The white Jake Blount seeks out the Negro Dr. Copeland because the two burn to reform their society. Both struggle with the unsolved problem of whether or not to use violence

---

20. *The Heart Is a Lonely Hunter*, p. 26.

and temporarily sacrifice the ends to the means. The source of the bitter hurt which drives them is the same; for Copeland "the hopeless suffering of his people made in him a madness, a wild and evil feeling of destruction," and for Jake "the sight of this poverty was so cruel and hopeless that [he] snarled and clenched his fists."[21] The two men wish to share their ideas and plans, but they quarrel fiercely. The barrier in their relationship is similarity rather than difference, and like all barriers it throws violence in the way of communication.

Because she is attracted by the countless forms of love, Mrs. McCullers necessarily portrays violence as a private rather than a public matter. She does not seek to explain warped personalities and twisted loves on the basis of environment or heritage. All that is certain, as the Macy brothers in *The Ballad of the Sad Café* illustrate, is the unpredictable nature of love. Abandoned by their parents but loved by their foster-mother, they develop opposite temperaments. Henry becomes patient and shy, easily touched by the misfortunes of others; Marvin turns rough and cruel, a center of violence. For the most part in Mrs. McCullers' fiction problems of the present occupy the stage to the exclusion of the past, and the author does not search for explanations in history as does Faulkner. Nor does she prepare a broad condemnation of modern society, except in relation to race. Thus when J. T. Malone feels that he is blundering about in a world incapable of order, he is not drawing conclusions about the world in general but is reflecting the alteration which approaching death makes in his perception of reality. Again, the reflections in the golden eye of the fire are "tiny and grotesque," the misery of an isolated group of people. Mrs. McCullers makes no attempt to prove that the experiences which she portrays are prototypes of specifically modern behavior; she is content simply to make vivid the violence of the psychological and physiological illnesses that result from thwarted or abnormal love.

Although treating a subject close to Eudora Welty's theme

21. *Ibid.*, p. 27.

of love and isolation, Mrs. McCullers uses violence less as a revelation to the characters involved than as an external description of their condition. There is a minimum of exposition of the unconscious. Most of the characters, except the adolescents and the psychotics, can identify their emotions and evaluate their connection with other people. Mrs. McCullers prefers direct reporting of tension and violence to the ambivalence of fantasy which Miss Welty develops. She also treats grotesque characters objectively and matter-of-factly. In *The Ballad of the Sad Café* she uses a device like the folk narrator to lengthen the aesthetic distance between the freakish characters and the reader. Events of violence in her fiction, however, always bring the reader in close to the narration.

In each of the novels an act of violence forms the climax in which tensions are not so much resolved as openly expressed and rearranged. New combinations of love will follow, but there is little or no indication that they will protect the characters from continuing conflict, for the complexities of love will inevitably provoke violence.

VIII. Primitives and violence: Shirley Ann Grau

Violence is a convincing inevitability in fiction by Shirley Ann Grau because it is inherent in her special material. The province of her best work is the primitive—people who are isolated by geography, occupation, poverty, and race. In her first novel and short stories she deals with the mixed Spanish and French people living on coastal islands and along bayous west of the three mouths of the Mississippi River and with Negroes in their subcommunity among Southern whites. The islanders belong to her in the same way that back-country folk of Florida belong to Marjorie Kinnan Rawlings or the hill people of Kentucky to Elizabeth Madox Roberts. Although Miss Grau's island people lack the subtle complicated social code which shaped Cable's Creole characters, they adhere to customs and principles sanctioned by years of repetition. This body of tradition is a core of stability within a volatile community where the hazards of fishing, the heat and the storms, and the oppressive isolation breed violence. These conditions are detailed in *The Hard Blue Sky* (1958), an episodic novel devoted to the islanders. In *The Black Prince* (1955), a collection of short stories, she describes the conditions of violence among bayou folk, Negroes, and whites. In her second novel, *The House on Coliseum Street* (1961), she changes focus to relate the minutiae of a crisis within a single consciousness as Joan Mitchell's drifting through meaningless experiences recapitulates the almost stereotyped futility of modern life. Miss Grau's most recent novel, *The Keepers of the House* (1964), brings together intense private crises and the history of violence in the South in the voice of Abigail, who must defeat Wade County in order to defend her family.

Like other Southern writers, Miss Grau is an observer at first hand, having been born in New Orleans in 1929. She was graduated from Newcomb College with Phi Beta Kappa honors and pursued graduate work in English literature of the Renaissance and the seventeenth century at Tulane University. At present she lives in New Orleans with her husband, the writer James Kern Feibleman. Her work has been well received by critics and reviewers, and, possibly because of its objectivity, it has occasioned less unfavorable criticism than that of Truman Capote and William Goyen. In reviewing *The Black Prince,* William Peden summed up the quality characteristic especially of her first three books which sets them apart from the Gothic strain in Southern literature:

... she avoids sensationalism, violence, and whimsy for their own sakes. She writes out of neither sentimental love nor tear-filled despair. Hers is not a namby-pamby world of dreams, or a darkened alley in which animals die meaningless deaths. Frustration and violence and death are present in her world, but so also are serenity, achievement, and life. She has produced a world not haunted by victims of malignant destiny, but an essentially vibrant one lived in by human beings whom she reveals during moments of stress, crisis, or decision.[1]

The Keepers of the House moves in a new direction, letting the reportorial eye look into the burden of violence which the South has carried from its slaveholding past into miscegenation and contemporary destructiveness.

Miss Grau's forte is precise, clear reporting of selected details which give her fiction a circumstantial solidity reminiscent of the realism of Balzac or Flaubert. Each of her short stories begins with the facts of the setting, so that the environment takes on the quality of another character and lends its validity to that of the fictional people. Violence may inhere in the setting itself or it may develop in man's struggle to sustain life against natural forces as impersonal as those which surround the shipwrecked men in Stephen Crane's "The Open Boat." Having established the perspective of her picture, Miss Grau moves closer and records the conversations of her characters, often turning over to dialogue an entire narrative sequence with the authority of a Hemingway. But she may then return to the vantage point of the omniscient author and summarize and explain freely.

In the absence of indirection, half-lights, subterranean explorations, and involved imagery, her style is simple and straightforward. Most of her characters, for example, are uncomplicated, outgoing people whose actions are made violent more by circumstance than by flawed human nature. She apparently observes human beings with no purpose in mind except that of finding them interesting enough to record. This view in itself conveys a wholehearted acceptance and affirmation of mankind which finds a sort of low-key heroism in the refusal to whine, to grovel in self-pity, or to collapse in despair.

1. "Vibrant World" (review of *The Black Prince and Other Stories*), *Saturday Review*, XXXVIII (Jan. 29, 1955), 16.

Miss Grau tells stories as happenings and events. The surface is important because that is where action occurs. Details of sight, sound, and movement vivify the surface, but often these parts, although related, are not shaped into a single design by a theme. Without this control the incidents tend to be documentary rather than imaginative, to record rather than to interpret. An element like violence, then, appears chiefly as a fact inscribed to preserve the accuracy of the scene. It lacks the urgency which it has when treated as an agent of destiny or moral revelation or social criticism. By concentrating on a description of the primitive in the sense of geographical and intellectual isolation, Miss Grau is likely to oversimplify human relationships.

In *The House on Coliseum Street* she began for the first time to portray the complexities of love, which may free or imprison the human spirit in proportion to the person's willingness to take the risk of loving others. This exploration continues in *The Keepers of the House* in which she probes the struggle for power and the demands of love that offer man his moments for moral grandeur or cowardice. She is too well aware of the frustrations, dangers, and violence of the elemental to lapse into sentimentality or false glamour. Her characters work hard to provide food for families and to keep houses repaired, to discipline children and to find some leisure. They are not romantics ennobled by humanitarian impulses or by the beauty of nature. Often, in fact, the environment is another opponent to be outmaneuvered or defeated.

The novel in which Miss Grau treats nature most fully as a violent protagonist is *The Hard Blue Sky*. Isle aux Chiens with its wild dogs, trees burned by salt spray and twisted by wind, and almost impenetrable thickets of wisteria and bougainvillea seems scarcely habitable. "The wind and the Gulf together," one of the characters thinks, "could lift it right off and scatter it all up and down the coast in a million billion pieces."[2] Nor is the marsh north of the harbor any less a threat

2. *The Hard Blue Sky* (New York: Alfred A. Knopf, 1958), p. 206.

to the islanders. Under the shiny motionless surface of the water which is impervious to the gaze of man lie various forms of natural violence: alligators, sharp-toothed eels, and snakes with venom which kills strong men within three hours. The fact that the only deaths in the novel occur when human beings invade the interior of the "prairie tremblant" points up the catastrophe which waits at the edge of these lives. Henry Livaudais fails when he elopes with a Yugoslav girl from the rival island Terre Haute and attempts to cross the swamp to escape possible pursuers. His father reconstructs the death of the pair by thinking first of the cottonmouth moccasin that caught them, and then imagining the body of the girl, who must have been beautiful, disintegrating as the insects and fishes worked at it. The omnipresent aggression of nature even intrudes as the men sit smoking with the grieving father; each time one drops a cigarette into the water, a fish flashes up to strike it. The only word they have for grief is to call Henry "crazy." They are inarticulate and resigned to conditions which they can neither change nor rail against effectively. Only a woman like Cecile Boudreau, who dreads the time when her infant son will be ready to go into the marsh, rebels against nature. Swearing in her despair at the death of Henry, she hurls a brick at the hard sky. The violence in the conflict between man and his environment which might flare in this novel is constantly held back by the simplicity of the islanders. They never dream of leaving their setting, and they feel nothing personal in the blows which they suffer.

Throughout the narrative the threat of a September hurricane hangs in the glassy, overheated days and in the memories of those who have survived such storms. All the tensions of the late summer both among the people and in the atmosphere seem to find a purpose in the preparations for the storm. Annie, an adolescent who thinks she wants to leave the island for New Orleans, has gone off with the visiting outlander. Those who remain are devoted to the island and get ready "to save what they can and lose what they must" as they had for generations.[3] The novel ends just as the winds strike, for the storm would be an anticlimax to the waiting and the preparations. Furthermore, in the memories of Hector Boudreau and of Mamere Terrebonne, the oldest woman on the island, the terrors of hurricanes have already been counted over, so that a new record is unnecessary.

The incipient violence of nature permeates all of Miss Grau's writing about the Gulf Coast, for the marsh and water and wind are implacably unyielding to the presence of man. And over everything burns the sun which crazes those who remain in it too long. In the story "Joshua" the child Joshua knows that the one man who tried to cross the swamp off Goose Bayou never reappeared. Even though the man was white, the Negroes hunted for two days to kill him for assaulting and murdering one of their girls, but by going into the swamp he, like Henry Livaudais, in effect committed suicide. The marsh is an unchanging threat, perpetually fresh; even after a hurricane the grasses spring back undamaged, as the author notes in another story of the bayous, "The Way of a Man." This persistent strain of the magnitude and power of natural forces in Miss Grau's work achieves an almost naturalistic reduction of the status of man to a biological cipher insignificant among other forms of life. But the pessimistic attitude which is the logical consequence of this view is expressed only once by Miss Grau's characters and is never acted upon. Angry and despairing over the loss of Henry Livaudais, Cecile Boudreau says, "It don't even matter that we been alive"; but her response is not typical among people who customarily accommodate themselves to violence in nature or in their occupations without making histrionic protests.[4] In the long run, the heavy heat, the glare of the sun, and the dust-laden winds compose a dense atmosphere which dulls rather than sharpens the violence. In some circumstances the physi-

3. *Ibid.*, p. 428.
4. *Ibid.*, p. 286.

cal world seems to encumber conflict and action until they occur only in slow motion.

In addition to the violence which rises from the primitive environment in her first two books, Miss Grau portrays the violence of the tribe in isolated communities like Isle aux Chiens. Here the authority of parents is direct and vigorous. The young children who swarm over the island are disciplined by force. Marie Livaudais punishes six-year-old Robby by roughly washing his mouth with strong soap and thundering at him that his tongue will drop out with cancer and that she will break his teeth like acorns. Sixteen-year-old Annie Landry is dragged home by her father who threatens to whip her unless she apologizes for insulting her stepmother. The authority of the husband and the subservience of the wife clash when Hector, remembering the horrors of previous hurricanes, tries to force Cecile to leave the house and come with him when the boats are taken to safety. The two fight until Hector goes out, leaving behind Cecile hissing at his threats that he will kill her if the children are not safe when he returns. On the boat he grins with pride over her determination and lack of fear. This violence marks the bounds of order and respect within the family and the community. Its crudeness is a primitive communication of strength and security. These people preserve rather than destroy themselves through violence. By it they teach the children the terms of membership in the community, and they police their own integrity. Although their life is harsh and limited, it is not frustrating as it is for the tenant farmers in Caldwell or the degenerating land owners in Faulkner. The violence, therefore, is not a protest but a positive accommodation to a restrictive environment and occupation.

Because the isolated islanders suspect strangers, they are violent toward those who enter their grounds. When the crew of the *Bozo* scrape their boat against the *Pixie*, a sailboat from New Orleans temporarily brought into the island harbor,

Inky, left in charge of the *Pixie*, prepares to fight the *Bozo* crew. But there is an inexplicable change in the mood and the island men saunter off. During his few weeks on the island Inky is never subjected to personal violence except once when mistaken for a rival by one of the young men at a dance, but his ignorance of the courtesies of the island betrays him when on an occasion like the fire at the Landry house, he fails to come to ask about Annie.

Like families on the frontier, the islanders engage in the ritualistic violence of a feud. National pride and a sense of vocational superiority set the French and Spanish shrimp fishermen of Isle aux Chiens against the Yugoslav oyster fishermen and the trappers on the neighboring island Terre Haute. Violences have been exchanged between the two sets of islanders for years—fighting when the two groups meet on the mainland, stealing oysters, setting fires on the beaches, and shooting from boats. These culminate in a devastating outbreak when Pete Livaudais burns Terre Haute and shoots at the inhabitants for their remote connection with his brother's death in the swamp. Retaliation from the Terre Haute islanders destroys property on Isle aux Chiens, but more importantly it makes changes in the relationships of the Landry family. As they fight to save their house, Adele, the stepmother, proves her strength and resourcefulness, Annie asserts her independence by calling her father by his first name, and Inky loses favor by failing to inquire about Annie. Miss Grau constructs these large scenes with skill, choosing the flash of light, the sound of a voice, the howl of a dog, the rush of spectators which fall together in patterns that break and change like the bits in a kaleidoscope until the violence is multiplied by being reflected from every angle of the setting.

In a story like "The Black Prince" in which the protagonist is Stanley Albert, a fine black incarnation of Lucifer, feuding breaks out around the central figure as easily as he mints money from wax. A genuine agent of evil, he makes the men jealous because the women admire his unusual wealth, and he watches unscathed while they injure and kill one another in lieu of battling Stanley Albert himself. His distance from the action is part of the folklore fantasy of the entire story and converts the violence into an illustration of the catalystic nature of a principle of evil which seems to release rather than to generate the deadly sins of the characters.

Most of the episodes involving the bayou folk in Miss Grau's fiction stress the singularity of the kind of life which their isolation has led them to develop and the violence which develops from this separateness. But in the story of Annie Landry's growing up which is woven into *The Hard Blue Sky*, Miss Grau emphasizes the psychological experiences that are typical of the adolescent in contemporary fiction. Like Frankie Addams in *The Member of the Wedding* and Joel Knox in *Other Voices, Other Rooms* she has suffered the loss of a parent. This withdrawal of guidance increases the adolescent's natural uncertainty and tensions. Miss Grau catches the nightmarish quality of Annie's life, disturbed as the girl is by grief for her mother and by maturing sexual desires. Her ominous dreams and startled midnight awakenings, her sudden forays into the jungle tangles on the island, and her impulsive fishing expeditions suggest the hidden violence of her undirected energy which makes it difficult for her to live with herself or others. She is sent to an Ursuline convent in New Orleans where, to her, the most important event is her attempt to watch her South American roommate meet a lover on the school grounds. The danger and the shimmering unreal quality of her climb along an upper-story ledge on a convent building at night seem like an enactment of her bad dreams, a remarkable sensuous representation of a disturbed psychological state. In keeping with the primitivism of her community on the island, Annie assumes an adult role early. By the end of the novel she has forced her father and stepmother to accept her decisions; she has been seduced; and she has chosen to leave the island for New Orleans. The independence of the islanders means that the community accords Annie an equal independence and in effect exposes her to violence from which a character like Frankie Addams is held back.

A more conventional portrait of adolescence appears in the short story "The Longest Day" in which the adolescent Patsy violently struggles against the boredom of her day.[5] With all the anger and brattishness of one of Flannery O'Connor's child characters, the girl threatens to kill a neighbor's daughter, deliberately ruins her own clothes, and verbally assaults her family. Miss Grau seems to assume that readers now are well trained in understanding the motivation of adolescents, so that her only purpose is to record the manifest violence. Because it is the situation in *The Hard Blue Sky* and the formula in "The Longest Day" which hold these stories together, not any intrinsically interesting characters, violence in these accounts of adolescence is less revealing and consequential than in the stories of initiation and development by Eudora Welty and Carson McCullers.

In Miss Grau's first fiction the Negro is largely another primitive whose violence expresses uninhibited passions and temper. The relationship of Negro and white does not occupy Miss Grau here. In only one story does the peculiar social status of the Negro directly play a part; therefore, the kind of violence which is a statement of social criticism by reflecting biracial competition, injustice, and hatred is absent. In its place Miss Grau depicts the violence of personal relationships among Negroes. That she can subtly combine the public and the private violence of Negro life is evident in "Miss Yellow Eyes." The courage and ambition of light-skinned Chris, who plans to leave New Orleans and "pass" in Oregon once he returns from the Korean War, is played off against the cowardice and jealousy of Pete, who injures his hand to avoid war service. Pete torments his beautiful sister Lena, who marries Chris, by cynically pointing out that Chris "ain't good enough for white people, but sure good enough to get killed."[6] Later

5. "The Longest Day," *The New Yorker*, XXXI (Sept. 3, 1955), 30-34.
6. *The Black Prince and Other Stories* (New York: Alfred A. Knopf, 1955), p. 102.

when a telegram confirms that Chris's wounds have been fatal, Pete gloats, "Being white and fine, where it got you? Where it got you? Dead and rotten."[7] The mother repudiates her only son, and Lena fights by hurling a framed picture of their father against his stub of an arm. The unexpected violence of Lena and her mother emphasizes their pride and integrity and underscores the cravenness of Pete, strengths and weaknesses put to special tests by the circumstances of race.

Violence as a code to live by governs the actions of the Negroes Jayson, Joe, and Mannie in "White Girl, Fine Girl." The trio, working under the protection of Mannie's job as chauffeur for Senator Winkerton's family, had been successful bootleggers until Mannie's wife Aggie slept with Jayson. In the fight which followed, Jayson killed Mannie and seriously injured Joe. These events are recalled in the story when Jayson has been released from prison and has returned to see Aggie. She, however, has taken up violence in her own way by training her daughters to stone any man who comes to the house. Jayson defies her defenses and enters the house to wreck it as Grandfather Samuels ruined his son's home in "The White Rooster." The physical destruction signifies the end of Jayson's relationship with Aggie, and he stumbles off to find the almost white girl whom Joe has promised him and possibly to join another bootlegging enterprise. The violence apparently is self-perpetuating and the cycle is to begin again.

Usually Miss Grau limits herself to the observable fact, but in the short story "The Black Prince" she mixes myth and actuality in a fantasy reminiscent of *The Robber Bridegroom*. This is the story by Miss Grau which justifies John Nerber's comment that she and Miss Welty "have an essential sense of mystery, a special awareness and belief in invisible things."[8] In her fantasies Miss Welty uses violence to characterize the environment, the larger-than-life qualities of the actors, and the legendary prowess of their action. Miss Grau lets violence

7. *Ibid.*, p. 113.
8. "Violent and Gentle" (review of *The Black Prince and Other Stories*), *New York Times Book Review*, Jan. 16, 1955, p. 4.

define the magic of the Black Prince. At first he appears to be simply an extraordinarily agile fighter who defeats four men in one night at Willie's café. Subsequent violence begins to create the mystery of Stanley Albert. When Cy Mastern is killed and his house burned in one of the feuds which flare up as if Stanley Albert touched a match to tinder, Ed Stevens notices that the water Stanley Albert carried to the fire acted like kerosene: "Wherever he'd toss a bucketful, the fire would shoot up, brighter and hotter than before."[9] The newcomer violently establishes his right to sit in the café every night of the week by kicking in the front door when he finds the building locked. Stories of the rapidity with which he and Alberta, the girl he has won with his money and power, travel across the country puzzle the crossroads community. And Willie vows that the two once hurriedly sailed out a window in the café. The supernatural dimension is proved when Pete Stokes shoots through Stanley Albert's head and merely chips the wall behind. Finally Stanley Albert can be dispatched only through a form of magic violence that recalls *The Emperor Jones.* Willie molds bullets from the silver coins with which Stanley Albert had bought drinks at the café and wounds him. The pair are never seen again, but they remain in folk memory as the cause of every catastrophe from boll weevils to still-births. In telling such a folk story Miss Grau emphasizes the human need to shape the inexplicable hazards of life into form and meaning. The Prince of Blackness seduces by his promise of coin and comfort and destroys by his violence, yet his dominion persists even though man undoes one embodiment of evil. Stanley Albert represents the pleasure, leisure, luxury, and wealth which—in the equation of ambivalence formulated by Wilbur J. Cash—the Southerner as a hedonist relishes and the Southerner as a Puritan fears. Miss Grau uses the primitivistic simplicity of her characters to make this point with new freshness, but she does not violate their naïveté by treating it with condescension. She maintains the folk idiom

9. *The Black Prince,* p. 57.

throughout the story and makes the violence a literary adjunct of the fantasy.

The elemental person taking the shape of his environment like an amoeba appears again in *The House On Coliseum Street,* but here the elemental is a form of neuroticism and the violence is psychological. Unlike Miss Grau's preceeding books, this novel is introspective and faintly weary in tone. The motionless heat and the sick-smelling damp of a New Orleans summer parallel the miasmic life of the characters. Whatever might have been vital in the family on Coliseum Street has now become vulgar self-indulgence. Joan Mitchell, one of the five daughters produced by Aurelie Caillet's five marriages, floats on the decisions of her mother or on the passivity of her own personality. Her purposeless existence is a stasis from which she remarks, "It's hell to be alive, but it would be hell to be dead too."[10] After an abortion, she enacts in her life the death of her fetal child. She withdraws from reality and substitutes for it the sharp observation of scattered details. Miss Grau's skill in making hard and clear descriptions gives the dissociation of Joan the circumstantial vividness of a dream which cannot be forgotten. The stages of Joan's revenge evolve without conscious choice on her part; she spies on Michael Kern, breaks up another of his affairs by an anonymous letter, and finally destroys his teaching career. She has exorcised the evil and can now begin to forget. The destruction of Kern frees her from the valueless, empty life of the house on Coliseum Street, a consequence she had not anticipated. When she returns from the interview which will ruin Kern, the knob of the door to the locked house turns uselessly, and she waits on the front porch to watch the sun come up.

With Abigail Howland Mason Tolliver in *The Keepers of the House,* Miss Grau discovers demonic energy and purpose unknown to the inhabitants of the house on Coliseum Street.

10. *The House on Coliseum Street* (New York: Alfred A. Knopf, 1961), p. 52.

The first William Howland had returned from the Battle of New Orleans to claim a farm on the ridges above Providence River in Wade County. Successive generations of Howlands, always a William among them, bought more land, added slaves, and prospered, especially during wars. Abigail's grandfather became the wealthiest man in the state when World War II made his timber land invaluable, but he lived modestly like an upcountry farmer. Abigail saw him use his influence and courtliness only once when he forced her reinstatement at college after she had been expelled for engineering the elopement of a classmate.

Most of Abigail's reminiscences recall the festivals, the ceremonies, and the routines of Southern family life: the weddings which spilled aunts and uncles and cousins into Howland Place and the overflow into Madison City; the hunts on foot when the whites shot nothing and got drunk and the Negroes clubbed coons to death; the death of Grandfather Howland's young wife and son; and the yearly cycle of cotton planting and picking and hog killing. For three quarters of the novel the granddaughter's voice weaves together the fate of the family. Abigail herself enters as a child brought back to Howland Place when her father returned to England in 1939. She grows up with Margaret, the Negro woman invited to the house by William, and their children Robert, Nina, and Crissy. Margaret, whose father was white, sends her light-skinned children away to school in the North, where they are expected to remain. Abigail marries John Tolliver of the Tolliver Nation in Somerset County, a man whose resoluteness and concentration frighten Abigail. She bears John's children, forgives her husband's infidelities, visits hospitals, and drinks tea with the governor's wife. In the process of learning to be the wife of the next candidate for governor, Abigail realizes that John has used her from the beginning to build his political empire just as he had joined the Citizens Council and the Klan to insure votes.

The passivity of Abigail which seldom asked questions and

learned chiefly by osmosis suddenly bursts into hate for the opportunism of John and fear of the ghost of Margaret. Margaret's children reappear in Abigail's life, Nina to show off her unmistakably Negro husband from Philadelphia, Robert to boast about his white wife and his career, and Crissy to write from Paris, "the haven of American Negroes."[11] The only explanation which Abigail has is that they feel guilty for their mixed blood, and doubting that black can equal white, they lack the courage to make the life to which Margaret had given them up.

Abigail herself needs special courage when John's opponents reveal that William Howland and Margaret had been legally married in Cleveland. A casual arrangement of master and mistress the family and county had accepted; a marriage they repudiate. Abigail rises to defend both Margaret and William, recognizing at last that what she had learned from them was respect, integrity, strength, and love stronger than self-satisfaction. None of this order is visible to the white men who burn the barn and threaten to fire the house. Abigail assesses the violence of her neighbors coldly and without heroics: "Aimless anger had burned a barn, had killed cats and steers and a couple of hounds. And all my courage had only fired a parking lot and pumped a load of birdshot into the side of the car."[12] She will divorce John, and she will send her children away to school, but she will remain to ruin the county through the power which she has inherited as property from her grandfather. The past joins her as the memory of the Howlands who had claimed the land and fought their way through the violence of neighbors and nature to have their own place. "I know," she admits, "that I shall hurt as much as I have been hurt." But she promises, "I shall destroy as much as I have lost."[13] The first step is to close the hotel in Madison City. Then she outlines her revenge to the women at the first

11. *The Keepers of the House* (New York: Alfred A. Knopf, 1964), p. 242.
12. *Ibid.*, p. 293.
13. *Ibid.*, p. 4.

tea to which she is invited after the barn burning, women who are the wives of the men who attacked Howland Place. She will sell the cattle which sustain the slaughterhouse and the ice-cream plant; she will fail to renew contracts for the lumber business.

The new warfare will be between whites, between the middle-class owner of resources and the middle-class processors of those resources. Abigail will fight out of hatred for her own who have turned against her and out of love for the house and the land. Margaret's children and the local Negroes are really on the edge of the storm, having been used to set it in motion but having little to do with its course. The Howlands who have made their own rules for life in the South are finally defended by a woman who acts by instinct in a primitive fierceness which leaves her crying on the floor of her husband's office, "huddled fetus-like against the cold unyielding boards."[14] The protection which their men and customs have supplied the Howland women (and the South) has now been ripped away and the exposed person craves vengeance. There is nothing liberating about the vengeance which will destroy the livelihood of the citizens of the county as well as the soul of Abigail, who thinks of herself as the keeper of the house. She foreshadows the end of the Gothic in ruins over which there will be none to sing except perhaps the Negroes who have escaped to the North.

This novel may presage a new use of the old blood theme. Here its violence visits the innocent white who acts to defend, not to expiate. Only those who deny the integrity of the relationship of William Howland and Margaret feel guilty or afraid. For the first time there is a counterattack which is undertaken deliberately to preserve the land by the economic power derived from the land. The battle is for the ultimate reality, that of being a person among persons. Miss Grau sees the physical details of the conflict with unimpeded sharpness. The meaning of the externals when taken into the characters,

14. *Ibid.*, p. 309.

however, is less sharp. The simplicity of the islanders in *The Hard Blue Sky* matches the straight, hard lines of their daily life, but the simplicity of Abigail Tolliver borders on insensibility in the face of racial and regional antagonisms. She can recall in lyrical tones the beauty of white jasmine and cherokee roses or relate clinically the birth of a child. But the narrating voice lacks the meditation necessary to reach meaning in complications like those of the Howlands.

Miss Grau's attitude toward her material governs the use which she makes of violence in her fiction. Working largely without a dominant theme or an explicit philosophical view, she approaches violence as another element typically present in the lives she records. She is not tempted like Erskine Caldwell to exploit her primitives for the sake of social or economic theories. Miss Grau stays outside as an observer and only rarely permits a character to become introspective and subtly analytical. The basis of her observation is a profound respect for the integrity of any manner or condition of human life. For this reason her primitive characters rarely think of themselves as dispossessed, unfortunate, oppressed, and unloved. They have few illusions about life and face it as a struggle against uncertainty, anxiety, fear, danger, poverty, and death, but they do not consider it a terror. There is no need for the distortions of grotesqueness to express spiritual maladjustments or to convey a sense of horror because the characters are generally reconciled to the terms of reality. For all the shock and violence which inhere in the natural surroundings where they earn a livelihood and build their homes, they find life worth living; or if such a positive deduction cannot be made, at least neither the author nor they question whether it is worth living.

In her novel of urban life the characters are neurotic persons unrelated to their environment or to other persons. Miss Grau portrays their rootlessness in terms which are familiar in mid-century literature. They court self-destruction. They feed on sensations moment by moment without thinking them into meanings which can be retained. Their violence denotes anxiety, frustration, and insecurity. The spirit of the Southern family has declined from a unifying concern to a series of warring desires. If a simple equation were to be drawn it would link weakness with the city where man is anonymous and strength with the island where man perforce reckons with the natural world and where he trusts his community.

Despite her highly developed sense of the actual and her precise record of the visible, Miss Grau represents a new romanticism which cultivates the isolated and the out-of-the-way. Like a local color writer but one entirely free from the mannerisms of quaintness she preserves in her stories of the Louisiana coast the ways of people remote from the contemporary South. The mood is keyed to the lethargy of a steamy, languid atmosphere. The characters are new innocents in modern literature. They express themselves in action rather than thought not because they are depraved, irrational, or decadent beings but because they are both vigorously human and animal. Their lives are relatively unaffected by institutions like church and school, which formalize and give continuity to the passage of time. They seem to light a candle at church and call on a voodoo woman with equal faith. Because they have never been part of the mainstream of Southern history, their violence is not an accumulation of complications from the past carried into the present as a loss of order or a sense of guilt as it appears in the meditations of William Faulkner or Robert Penn Warren. Their past is Jean Lafitte and the family's fishing record, and the present consists of little more than the unchanged daily routine. Social changes such as industrialization and urbanization have not touched them. For these people New Orleans represents activities which geographically are not so very distant but which culturally are entirely removed from them. The Negroes of New Orleans or upcountry Alabama live closer to the dominant white society than do the coastal people, but they are separated from it by social and economic strictures. In the few stories dealing with the ordinary white community Miss Grau focuses on characters set apart by pride or adolescence. The pride of the Howlands, savage and oblivious of consequences, is called crazy by outsiders. It has so fully supported the two Abigails that they have seldom had to think. It has protected them from doubting the ways of their family and from self-examination. They live by absorbing the certainty of the life of Margaret and William without reflecting on its singularity.

Although these forms of isolation foster distinctive habits of life, they also become a bridge to the treatment of universal problems and reactions. When Miss Grau portrays characters like the bayou and island people whose lives are structured by the natural elements from which they take food and shelter, she sketches the primal roots of all human experience. The violence of this experience is chiefly physical rather than psychological, active rather than contemplative. By it she marks man's place in nature, depicting a direct relationship which has become increasingly rare in a mechanized world. At the same times she denies the romantic thesis that the elemental man is a free agent protected by his environment, for she stresses the violence of nature which assails him. And finally she creates a character like Abigail who is willing to fight the violence of the human hearts turned against her, doing violence herself because "it had to be done."

Postnote

Major Southern writers of fiction during the past two decades have made the violent and the grotesque powerful vehicles of their perception of reality. We stand too near in time to know whether these twenty years complete one literary movement or whether they introduce another. In terms of simple quantity, the younger writers like Shirley Ann Grau describe less violence than do older writers like Robert Penn Warren. Inevitably, new writers will hunt their own directions. Just as it is possible to detect differences in the use of violence by Southern writers before and after 1940, so it is probable that other differences will develop in the work of writers who will come after those discussed here. The very vitality of the achievement which the newcomers will inherit will compel them to be original. As Flannery O'Connor remarked about the influence of Faulkner, "nobody wants his mule and wagon stalled on the same track when the Dixie Limited is roaring down."

At the present time an evaluation of the achievement of recent Southern writers in using violence reveals the significance which they have given this mode. In style they have extracted forceful literary effects from violence and grotesqueness. For the density secured by Faulkner and Wolfe by luxuriant vocabulary and involved syntax, the younger writers depend largely upon metaphors and symbols. These devices condense the narration but expand its allusiveness, thus moving in the direction of poetry. On another level the rhythms of Southern dialectal speech and the pungency of folk words have a peculiar tone and roughness appropriate to statements of violence or grotesqueness. Distortion, which gives scope both to literary and to folk language, ranges from the robust lyricism of Faulkner to the radiant lyricism of Goyen, from the twang of backwoods people in Warren and O'Connor to the sophisticated reasoning of jaded moderns in Styron and Grau, from quasi-naturalistic reporting in Caldwell to romance in Welty, from lament in Wolfe to laughter in Capote.

Living in the period before and after World War II, these writers in the South have seen factories spread over farmland and have watched country towns grow into cities and cities into national centers of population. They have observed the accelerated movement of people to and from the region. They may indeed be witnesses to the end of the South as a region of manners distinguishable from those of other sections. The destructive and antiheroic impulses accompanying the changes can be discharged in literary violence which takes on meaning from the writers' prior faith in order.

Although each author writes about the South which he knows and which therefore differs from that presented by others, each expresses or implies the existence of a moral and a social order from which man diverges at the risk of destroying himself, his family, and his community. Their characters are not mere biological ciphers living and dying in a succession of involuntary reactions. They may often be distorted, but there are points of meaning from which their distortion departs or toward which it leads. The writers depict confusion and turmoil as typical of the course between these points. But they do not despair. They make sense out of distortion and dislocation. By converting these extremes into literature, they dramatize the power of order; they make its absence painful and give purpose to the anguish of trying to achieve it.

Acknowledgments

Permission to quote from the following works is gratefully acknowledged:
From *In Search of Heresy: American Literature in an Age of Conformity.*
Copyright 1956. McGraw-Hill Book Company. Used by permission.

From *Call It Experience: The Years of Learning How to Write* (copyright 1951); *Georgia Boy* (copyright 1942); *Journeyman* (copyright 1935); *Tragic Ground* (copyright 1944); and *Trouble in July* (copyright 1940) by Erskine Caldwell. Reprinted by permission of Little, Brown and Company.

From *The Grass Harp* (copyright 1951); *Other Voices, Other Rooms* (copyright 1948); and *A Tree of Night and Other Stories* (copyright 1945, 1946, 1947, 1948, 1949) by Truman Capote. Reprinted by permission of Random House, Inc.

From *Where Main Street Meets the River* by Hodding Carter. Copyright 1952, 1953. Reprinted by permission of Holt, Rinehart and Winston, Inc.

From *The Mind of the South* by William J. Cash. Copyright 1941. Reprinted by permission of Alfred A. Knopf, Inc.

From *Absalom, Absalom!* (copyright 1951); *Big Woods* (copyright 1931, 1940, 1942, 1951, 1955); *Go Down, Moses and Other Stories* (copyright 1942); *Sanctuary* (copyright 1931); *The Hamlet* (copyright 1931, 1936, 1940); and *The Sound and the Fury & As I Lay Dying* (copyright 1929, 1930, 1946) by William Faulkner. Reprinted by permission of Random House, Inc.

From *The Romantic Comedians* by Ellen Glasgow. Copyright 1926. Doubleday, Page & Company. Reprinted by permission of the estate of Ellen Glasgow.

From *The Faces of Blood Kindred: A Novella and Ten Stories* (copyright 1960); *Ghost and Flesh* (copyright 1947, 1951, 1952); *The House of Breath* (copyright 1949, 1950); and *In a Farther Country* (copyright 1955) by William Goyen. Reprinted by permission of the author.

From *The Fair Sister* by William Goyen. Copyright 1963 by William Goyen. Reprinted by permission of Doubleday & Company, Inc.

From *The Black Prince and Other Stories* (copyright 1955); *The Hard Blue Sky* (copyright 1958); *The House on Coliseum Street* (copyright 1961); and *The Keepers of the House* (copyright 1964) by Shirley Ann Grau. Reprinted by permission of Alfred A. Knopf, Inc.

From *The Ballad of the Sad Café* (copyright 1951); *Clock Without Hands* (copyright 1961); *The Heart Is a Lonely Hunter* (copyright 1940); *The Member of the Wedding* (copyright 1946); and *Reflections in a Golden Eye* (copyright 1941) by Carson McCullers. Reprinted by permission of Houghton Mifflin Company.

From *A Good Man Is Hard To Find* by Flannery O'Connor. Copyright 1953, 1954, 1955. Reprinted by permission of Harcourt, Brace & World, Inc.

From *The Violent Bear It Away* (copyright 1955, 1960) and *Wise Blood* (copyright 1949, 1952) by Flannery O'Connor. Reprinted by permission of Farrar, Straus & Company, Inc.

From *Everything That Rises Must Converge.* Copyright © The Estate of Mary Flannery O'Connor, 1956, 1957, 1958, 1960, 1961, 1962, 1964, 1965. Reprinted by permission of the publisher, Farrar, Straus and Giroux, Inc.

From "The Fiction Writer and His Country" by Flannery O'Connor in *The Living Novel*, ed. Granville Hicks. Copyright 1957. Reprinted by permission of The Macmillan Company.

From *Lie Down in Darkness*, copyright 1951, by William Styron. Reprinted by permission of the publishers, The Bobbs-Merrill Company, Inc.

Index